WITHDRAWN

FEARLESS

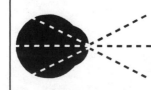

This Large Print Book carries the
Seal of Approval of N.A.V.H.

FEARLESS

IMAGINE YOUR LIFE WITHOUT FEAR

MAX LUCADO

THORNDIKE PRESS
A part of Gale, Cengage Learning

GALE
CENGAGE Learning

Detroit • New York • San Francisco • New Haven, Conn • Waterville, Maine • London

GALE
CENGAGE Learning˙

Copyright © 2009 by Max Lucado.
Thorndike Press, a part of Gale, Cengage Learning.
Permissions information on pages 5–6.

LIBRARY OF CONGRESS CATALOGING-IN-PUBLICATION DATA

Lucado, Max.
    Fearless : imagine your life without fear / by Max Lucado. —
Large print ed.
      p. cm. — (Thorndike Press large print inspirational)
    Includes bibliographical references.
    ISBN-13: 978-1-4104-2271-2 (hardcover : alk. paper)
    ISBN-10: 1-4104-2271-2 (hardcover : alk. paper)
    1. Fear—Religious aspects—Christianity. 2. Large type books.
I. Title.
BV4908.5.L83 2010
248.8'6—dc22   2009037660

Published in 2010 by arrangement with Thomas Nelson, Inc.

PERMISSIONS

All Scripture quotations, unless otherwise indicated, are taken from The New King James Version. © 1982 by Thomas Nelson, Inc. Used by permission. All rights reserved.

Other Scripture references are from the following sources:

The Amplifed Bible (AMP), Copyright © 1954, 1958, 1962, 1964, 1965, 1987 by The Lockman Foundation. Used by permission. The Contemporary English Version (CEV). © 1991 by the American Bible Society. Used by permission. *The Message* (MSG) by Eugene H. Peterson. © 1993, 1994, 1995, 1996, 2000. Used by permission of NavPress Publishing Group. All rights reserved. New American Standard Bible® (NASB), © The Lockman Foundation 1960, 1962, 1963, 1968, 1971, 1972, 1973, 1975, 1977, 1995. Used by permission. New

For Dee
and all who loved him

CONTENTS

ACKNOWLEDGMENTS 11

1. Why Are We Afraid? 13
2. The Villagers of Stiltsville 33
   Fear of Not Mattering

3. God's Ticked Off at Me 49
   Fear of Disappointing God

4. Woe, Be Gone 65
   Fear of Running Out

5. My Child Is in Danger 81
   Fear of Not Protecting My Kids

6. I'm Sinking Fast 99
   Fear of Overwhelming Challenges

7. There's a Dragon in My Closet . . 115
   Fear of Worst-Case Scenarios

8. This Brutal Planet 133
   Fear of Violence

9. Make-Believe Money 147
   Fear of the Coming Winter

10. Scared to Death 165
   Fear of Life's Final Moments

11. Caffeinated Life. 179
   Fear of What's Next

12. The Shadow of a Doubt 193
   Fear That God Is Not Real

13. What If Things Get Worse? . . . 211
   Fear of Global Calamity

14. The One Healthy Terror 229
   Fear of God Getting Out of My Box

15. Conclusion 245
   William's Psalm

   DISCUSSION GUIDE 255
   NOTES 303

ACKNOWLEDGMENTS

If a book is a house, meet the construction crew behind this one. (Step out and take a bow as I call your name, please.)

Liz Heaney and Karen Hill, editors. Is this really our twenty-fifth book together? You two deserve gold medals. For the hundreds of chapters, thousands of nudges, and millions of happy moments — thank you.

Steve and Cheryl Green. The sun will forget to rise before you will fail to serve. I love you both.

Carol Bartley, copy editor. Turn you loose on the world, and it would be weedless. Great job.

Susan and Greg Ligon, David Moberg, and the entire Thomas Nelson team. You've tapped into the wellhead of creativity. I can't thank you enough.

David Drury, researcher. Every suggestion, timely. Every correction, appreciated.

David Treat, prayer partner. Quietly praying us through. So grateful.

Randy Frazee, senior minister. You and Rozanne have brought joy to our hearts and calm to our calendar. Welcome!

UpWords Ministry team. For managing the radio program, Web page, and correspondence and putting up with me, a standing ovation!

The Oak Hills Church, our spiritual family for twenty years. The best decades await us.

Jenna, Andrea, and Sara, our daughters. Each one of you made tangible contributions to this book. Chasing down passages, digging through sources. I'm bursting with pride. And Brett Bishop, welcome to the family! May God unload a truck of blessings on you and Jenna.

And my wife, Denalyn. The sight of heaven's angels won't surprise me. I've been married to one for twenty-seven years. I love you!

■ ■ ■ ■ ■

CHAPTER 1
WHY ARE WE
AFRAID?

■ ■ ■ ■ ■

Why are you fearful, O you of little faith?
— MATTHEW 8:26

You would have liked my brother. Everyone did. Dee made friends the way bakers make bread: daily, easily, warmly. Handshake — big and eager; laughter — contagious and volcanic. He permitted no stranger to remain one for long. I, the shy younger brother, relied on him to make introductions for us both. When a family moved onto the street or a newcomer walked onto the playground, Dee was the ambassador.

But in his midteen years, he made one acquaintance he should have avoided — a bootlegger who would sell beer to underage drinkers. Alcohol made a play for us both, but although it entwined me, it enchained him. Over the next four decades my brother drank away health, relationships, jobs, money, and all but the last two years of his life.

Who can say why resolve sometimes wins and sometimes loses, but at the age of fifty-four my brother discovered an aquifer of willpower, drilled deep, and enjoyed a season of sobriety. He emptied his bottles, stabilized his marriage, reached out to his children, and exchanged the liquor store for the local AA. But the hard living had taken its toll. Three decades of three-packs-a-day smoking had turned his big heart into ground meat.

On a January night during the week I began writing this book, he told Donna, his wife, that he couldn't breathe well. He already had a doctor's appointment for a related concern, so he decided to try to sleep. Little success. He awoke at 4:00 a.m. with chest pains severe enough to warrant a call to the emergency room. The rescue team loaded Dee onto the gurney and told Donna to meet them at the hospital. My brother waved weakly and smiled bravely and told Donna not to worry, but by the time she and one of Dee's sons reached the hospital, he was gone.

The attending physician told them the news and invited them to step into the room where Dee's body lay. Holding each other, they walked through the doors and saw his final message. His hand was resting on the top of his thigh with the two center fingers folded in and the thumb extended, the

16

universal sign-language symbol for "I love you."

I've tried to envision the final moments of my brother's earthly life: racing down a Texas highway in an ambulance through an inky night, paramedics buzzing around him, his heart weakening within him. Struggling for each breath, at some point he realized only a few remained. But rather than panic, he quarried some courage.

Perhaps you could use some. An ambulance isn't the only ride that demands valor. You may not be down to your final heartbeat, but you may be down to your last paycheck, solution, or thimble of faith. Each sunrise seems to bring fresh reasons for fear.

They're talking layoffs at work, slowdowns in the economy, flare-ups in the Middle East, turnovers at headquarters, downturns in the housing market, upswings in global warming, breakouts of al Qaeda cells. Some demented dictator is collecting nuclear warheads the way others collect fine wines. A strain of swine flu is crossing the border. The plague of our day, terrorism, begins with the word *terror*. News programs disgorge enough hand-wringing information to warrant an advisory: "Caution: this news report is best viewed in the confines of an underground vault in Iceland."

We fear being sued, finishing last, going broke; we fear the mole on the back, the new kid on the block, the sound of the clock as it ticks us closer to the grave. We sophisticate investment plans, create elaborate security systems, and legislate stronger military, yet we depend on mood-altering drugs more than any other generation in history. Moreover, "ordinary children today are more fearful than psychiatric patients were in the 1950s."[1]

Fear, it seems, has taken a hundred-year lease on the building next door and set up shop. Oversize and rude, fear is unwilling to share the heart with happiness. Happiness complies and leaves. Do you ever see the two together? Can one be happy and afraid at the same time? Clear thinking and afraid? Confident and afraid? Merciful and afraid? No. Fear is the big bully in the high school hallway: brash, loud, and unproductive. For all the noise fear makes and room it takes, fear does little good.

Fear never wrote a symphony or poem, negotiated a peace treaty, or cured a disease. Fear never pulled a family out of poverty or a country out of bigotry. Fear never saved a marriage or a business. Courage did that. Faith did that. People who refused to consult or cower to their timidities did that.

But fear itself? Fear herds us into a prison and slams the doors.

Wouldn't it be great to walk out?

Imagine your life wholly untouched by angst. What if faith, not fear, was your default reaction to threats? If you could hover a fear magnet over your heart and extract every last shaving of dread, insecurity, and doubt, what would remain? Envision a day, just one day, absent the dread of failure, rejection, and calamity. Can you imagine a life with no fear? This is the possibility behind Jesus' question.

"Why are you afraid?" he asks (Matt. 8:26 NCV).

At first blush we wonder if Jesus is serious. He may be kidding. Teasing. Pulling a quick one. Kind of like one swimmer asking another, "Why are you wet?" But Jesus doesn't smile. He's dead earnest. So are the men to whom he asks the question. A storm has turned their Galilean dinner cruise into a white-knuckled plunge.

Here is how one of them remembered the trip: "Jesus got into a boat, and his followers went with him. A great storm arose on the lake so that waves covered the boat" (Matt. 8:23–24 NCV).

These are Matthew's words. He remembered well the pouncing tempest and bouncing boat and was careful in his terminology. Not just any noun would do. He pulled his Greek thesaurus off the shelf and hunted for a descriptor that exploded like the waves across the bow. He bypassed common terms for spring shower, squall, cloudburst, or downpour. They didn't capture what he felt and saw that night: a rumbling earth and quivering shoreline. He recalled more than winds and whitecaps. His finger followed the column of synonyms down, down until he landed on a word that worked. "Ah, there it is." *Seismos* — a quake, a trembling eruption of sea and sky. "A great *seismos* arose on the lake."

The term still occupies a spot in our vernacular. A *seis*mologist studies earthquakes, a *seis*mograph measures them, and Matthew, along with a crew of recent recruits, felt a seismos that shook them to the core. He used the word on only two other occasions: once at Jesus' death when Calvary shook (Matt. 27:51–54) and again at Jesus' resurrection when the graveyard tremored (28:2). Apparently, the stilled storm shares equal billing in the trilogy of Jesus' great shake-ups: defeating sin on the cross, death at the tomb, and here silencing fear on the sea.

Sudden fear. We know the fear was sudden because the storm was. An older translation reads, "*Suddenly* a great tempest arose on the sea."

Not all storms come suddenly. Prairie farmers can see the formation of thunderclouds hours before the rain falls. This storm, however, springs like a lion out of the grass. One minute the disciples are shuffling cards for a midjourney game of hearts; the next they are gulping Galilean sea spray.

Peter and John, seasoned sailors, struggle to keep down the sail. Matthew, confirmed landlubber, struggles to keep down his breakfast. The storm is not what the tax collector bargained for. Do you sense his surprise in the way he links his two sentences? "Jesus got into a boat, and his followers went with him. A great storm arose on the lake" (8:23–24 NCV).

Wouldn't you hope for a more chipper second sentence, a happier consequence of obedience? "Jesus got into a boat. His followers went with him, and suddenly a great rainbow arched in the sky, a flock of doves hovered in happy formation, a sea of glass mirrored their mast." Don't Christ-followers enjoy a calendar full of Caribbean cruises? No. This story sends the not-so-subtle and not-too-popular reminder: getting on board with Christ can mean getting soaked with

Christ. Disciples can expect rough seas and stout winds. "In the world you will [not 'might,' 'may,' or 'could'] have tribulation" (John 16:33, brackets mine).

Christ-followers contract malaria, bury children, and battle addictions, and, as a result, face fears. It's not the absence of storms that sets us apart. It's whom we discover in the storm: an unstirred Christ.

"Jesus was sleeping" (v. 24 NCV).

Now there's a scene. The disciples scream; Jesus dreams. Thunder roars; Jesus snores. He doesn't doze, catnap, or rest. He slumbers. Could you sleep at a time like this? Could you snooze during a roller coaster loop-the-loop? In a wind tunnel? At a kettledrum concert? Jesus sleeps through all three at once!

Mark's gospel adds two curious details: "[Jesus] was in the stern, asleep on a pillow" (Mark 4:38). In the stern, on a pillow. Why the first? From whence came the second?

First-century fishermen used large, heavy seine nets for their work. They stored the nets in a nook that was built into the stern for this purpose. Sleeping *upon* the stern deck was impractical. It provided no space or protection. The small compartment beneath the stern, however, provided both.

22

It was the most enclosed and only protected part of the boat. So Christ, a bit dozy from the day's activities, crawled beneath the deck to get some sleep.

He rested his head, not on a fluffy feather pillow, but on a leather sandbag. A ballast bag. Mediterranean fishermen still use them. They weigh about a hundred pounds and are used to ballast, or stabilize, the boat.[2] Did Jesus take the pillow to the stern so he could sleep, or sleep so soundly that someone rustled him up the pillow? We don't know. But this much we do know. This was a premeditated slumber. He didn't accidentally nod off. In full knowledge of the coming storm, Jesus decided it was siesta time, so he crawled into the corner, put his head on the pillow, and drifted into dreamland.

His snooze troubles the disciples. Matthew and Mark record their responses as three staccato Greek pronouncements and one question.

The pronouncements: "Lord! Save! Dying!" (Matt. 8:25).

The question: "Teacher, do You not care that we are perishing?" (Mark 4:38).

They do not ask about Jesus' strength: "Can you still the storm?" His knowledge: "Are you aware of the storm?" Or his know-

23

how: "Do you have any experience with storms?" But rather, they raise doubts about Jesus' character: "Do you not care . . ."

Fear does this. Fear corrodes our confidence in God's goodness. We begin to wonder if love lives in heaven. If God can sleep in our storms, if his eyes stay shut when our eyes grow wide, if he permits storms after we get on his boat, does he care? Fear unleashes a swarm of doubts, anger-stirring doubts.

And it turns us into control freaks. "Do something about the storm!" is the implicit demand of the question. "Fix it or . . . or . . . or else!" Fear, at its center, is a perceived loss of control. When life spins wildly, we grab for a component of life we can manage: our diet, the tidiness of a house, the armrest of a plane, or, in many cases, people. The more insecure we feel, the meaner we become. We growl and bare our fangs. Why? Because we are bad? In part. But also because we feel cornered.

Martin Niemöller documents an extreme example of this. He was a German pastor who took a heroic stand against Adolf Hitler. When he first met the dictator in 1933, Niemöller stood at the back of the room and listened. Later, when his wife asked him what he'd learned, he said, "I discovered that Herr Hitler is a terribly frightened man."[3] Fear releases the tyrant within.

It also deadens our recall. The disciples had reason to trust Jesus. By now they'd seen him "healing all kinds of sickness and all kinds of disease among the people" (Matt. 4:23). They had witnessed him heal a leper with a touch and a servant with a command (Matt. 8:3, 13). Peter saw his sick mother-in-law recover (Matt. 8:14–15), and they all saw demons scatter like bats out of a cave. "He cast out the spirits with a word, and healed all who were sick" (Matt. 8:16).

Shouldn't someone mention Jesus' track record or review his résumé? Do they remember the accomplishments of Christ? They may not. Fear creates a form of spiritual amnesia. It dulls our miracle memory. It makes us forget what Jesus has done and how good God is.

And fear feels dreadful. It sucks the life out of the soul, curls us into an embryonic state, and drains us dry of contentment. We become abandoned barns, rickety and tilting from the winds, a place where humanity used to eat, thrive, and find warmth. No longer. When fear shapes our lives, safety becomes our god. When safety becomes our god, we worship the risk-free life. Can the safety lover do anything great? Can the risk-

25

averse accomplish noble deeds? For God? For others? No. The fear-filled cannot love deeply. Love is risky. They cannot give to the poor. Benevolence has no guarantee of return. The fear-filled cannot dream wildly. What if their dreams sputter and fall from the sky? The worship of safety emasculates greatness. No wonder Jesus wages such a war against fear.

His most common command emerges from the "fear not" genre. The Gospels list some 125 Christ-issued imperatives. Of these, 21 urge us to "not be afraid" or "not fear" or "have courage" or "take heart" or "be of good cheer." The second most common command, to love God and neighbor, appears on only eight occasions. If quantity is any indicator, Jesus takes our fears seriously. The one statement he made more than any other was this: don't be afraid.

Siblings sometimes chuckle at or complain about the most common command of their parents. They remember how Mom was always saying, "Be home on time," or, "Did you clean your room?" Dad had his favorite directives too. "Keep your chin up." "Work hard." I wonder if the disciples ever reflected on the most-often-repeated phrases of Christ. If so, they would have noted, "He was always calling us to courage."

So don't be afraid. You are worth much more than many sparrows. (Matt. 10:31 NCV)

Take courage, son; your sins are forgiven. (Matt. 9:2 NASB)

I tell you not to worry about everyday life — whether you have enough. (Matt. 6:25 NLT)

Don't be afraid. Just believe, and your daughter will be well. (Luke 8:50 NCV)

Take courage. I am here! (Matt. 14:27 NLT)

Do not fear those who kill the body but cannot kill the soul. (Matt. 10:28)

Do not fear, little flock, for it is your Father's good pleasure to give you the kingdom. (Luke 12:32)

Don't let your hearts be troubled. Trust in God, and trust also in me. . . . I will come and get you, so that you will always be with me where I am. (John 14:1, 3 NLT)

Don't be troubled or afraid. (John 14:27 NLT)

"Why are you frightened?" he asked. "Why are your hearts filled with doubt?" (Luke 24:38 NLT)

You will hear of wars and rumors of wars, but see to it that you are not alarmed. (Matt. 24:6 NIV)

Jesus came and touched them and said, "Arise, and do not be afraid." (Matt. 17:7)

Jesus doesn't want you to live in a state of fear. Nor do you. You've never made statements like these:

My phobias put such a spring in my step.

I'd be a rotten parent were it not for my hypochondria.

Thank God for my pessimism. I've been such a better person since I lost hope.

My doctor says if I don't begin fretting, I will lose my health.

We've learned the high cost of fear.

Jesus' question is a good one. He lifts his head from the pillow, steps out from the stern into the storm, and asks, "Why are you fearful, O you of little faith?" (Matt. 8:26).

To be clear, fear serves a healthy function. It is the canary in the coal mine, warning of potential danger. A dose of fright can keep a child from running across a busy road or an adult from smoking a pack of cigarettes. Fear is the appropriate reaction to a burning building or growling dog. Fear itself is not a sin. But it can lead to sin.

If we medicate fear with angry outbursts, drinking binges, sullen withdrawals, self-starvation, or viselike control, we exclude God from the solution and exacerbate the problem. We subject ourselves to a position of fear, allowing anxiety to dominate and define our lives. Joy-sapping worries. Day-numbing dread. Repeated bouts of insecurity that petrify and paralyze us. Hysteria is not from God. "For God has not given us a *spirit* of fear" (2 Tim. 1:7).

Fear may fill our world, but it doesn't have to fill our hearts. It will always knock on the door. Just don't invite it in for dinner, and for heaven's sake don't offer it a bed for the night. Let's embolden our hearts with a select number of Jesus' "do not fear" statements. The promise of Christ and the contention of this book are simple: we can fear less tomorrow than we do today.

When I was six years old, my dad let me stay up late with the rest of the family and watch the movie *The Wolf Man*. Boy, did he regret that decision. The film left me convinced that the wolf man spent each night prowling our den, awaiting his preferred meal of first-grade, redheaded, freckle-salted boy. My fear proved problematic. To reach the kitchen from my bedroom, I had to pass perilously close to his claws and fangs, something I was loath to do. More than once I retreated to my father's bedroom and awoke him. Like Jesus in the boat, Dad was sound asleep in the storm. *How can a person sleep at a time like this?*

Opening a sleepy eye, he would ask, "Now, why are you afraid?" And I would remind him of the monster. "Oh yes, the Wolf Man," he'd grumble. He would then climb out of bed, arm himself with super-human courage, escort me through the valley of the shadow of death, and pour me a glass of milk. I would look at him with awe and wonder, *What kind of man is this?*

Might it be that God views our seismos storms the way my father viewed my Wolf Man angst? "Jesus got up and gave a command to the wind and the waves, and it became completely calm" (Matt. 8:26 NCV).

He handles the great quaking with a great

calming. The sea becomes as still as a frozen lake, and the disciples are left wondering, "What kind of man is this? Even the winds and the waves obey him!" (v. 27 NCV).

What kind of man, indeed. Turning typhoon time into nap time. Silencing waves with one word. And equipping a dying man with sufficient courage to send a final love message to his family. Way to go, Dee. You faced your share of seismos moments in life, but in the end you didn't go under.

Here's a prayer that we won't either.

■ ■ ■ ■

CHAPTER 2
THE VILLAGERS
OF STILTSVILLE

■ ■ ■ ■

So don't be afraid. You are worth much more than many sparrows.

— MATTHEW 10:31 NCV

Fear of Not Mattering

Perhaps you don't know,
then, maybe you do,
about Stiltsville, the village,
(so strange but so true)

where people like we,
some tiny, some tall,
with jobs and kids
and clocks on the wall

keep an eye on the time.
For each evening at six,
they meet in the square
for the purpose of sticks,
tall stilts upon which

Stiltsvillians can strut
and be lifted above
those down in the rut:

the less and the least,

35

the Tribe of Too Smalls,
the not cools and have-nots
who want to be tall

but can't, because
in the giving of sticks,
their name was not called.
They didn't get picked.

Yet still they come
when villagers gather;
they press to the front
to see if they matter

to the clique of the cool,
the court of high clout,
that decides who is special
and declares with a shout,

"You're classy!" "You're pretty!"
"You're clever" or "Funny!"
And bequeath a prize,
not of medals or money,

not a freshly baked pie
or a house someone built,
but the oddest of gifts —
a gift of some stilts.

Moving up is their mission,

going higher their aim.
"Elevate your position"
is the name of their game.

The higher-ups of Stiltsville
(you know if you've been there)
make the biggest to-do
of the sweetness of thin air.

They relish the chance
on their high apparatus
to strut on their stilts,
the ultimate status.

For isn't life best
when viewed from the top?
Unless you stumble
and suddenly are not

so sure of your footing.
You tilt and then sway.
"Look out bel-o-o-o-w!"
and you fall straightaway

into the Too Smalls,
hoi polloi of the earth.
You land on your pride —
oh boy, how it hurts

when the chic police,

in the jilt of all jilts,
don't offer to help
but instead take your stilts.

"Who made you king?"
you start to complain
but then notice the hour
and forget your refrain.

It's almost six!
No time for chatter.
It's back to the crowd
to see if you matter.

Ah, there it is. There is the question. The
Amazon River out of which a thousand fears
flow: do we matter? We fear we don't. We
fear nothingness, insignificance. We fear
evaporation. We fear that in the last tabulation we make no contribution to the final
sum. We fear coming and going and no one
knowing.

That's why it bothers us when a friend
forgets to call or the teacher forgets our
name or a colleague takes credit for something we've done or the airline loads us like
cattle onto the next flight. They are affirm-
ing our deepest trepidation: no one cares,
because we aren't worth caring about. For
that reason we crave the attention of our

spouse or the affirmation of our boss, drop names of important people in conversations, wear college rings on our fingers, and put silicone in our breasts, flashy hubcaps on our cars, grids on our teeth, and silk ties around our necks. We covet some stilts.

Fashion designers tell us, "You'll be somebody if you wear our jeans. Stick our name on your rear end, and insignificance will vanish." So we do. And for a while we distance ourselves from the Too Smalls and enjoy a promotion into the Society of Higher-Ups. Fashion redeems us from the world of littleness and nothingness, and we are something else. Why? Because we spent half a paycheck on a pair of Italian jeans.

But then, horror of horrors, the styles change, the fad passes, the trend shifts from tight to baggy, faded to dark, and we're left wearing yesterday's jeans, feeling like yesterday's news. Welcome back to the Tribe of the Too Smalls.

Maybe we can outsource our insignificance. By coupling our identity with someone's Gulliver-sized achievement, we give our Lilliputian lives meaning. How else can you explain our fascination with sports franchises and athletes?

I am among the fascinated: an unabashed fan of the San Antonio Spurs. When they play basketball, I play basketball. When they score a basket, I score a basket. When they win, I dare to shout with the seventeen thousand other fans, "*We* won!" Yet how dare I make such a statement? Did I attend a single practice? Scout an opposing team? Contribute a coaching tip or sweat a drop of perspiration? No. I would if they asked. But I'm too insignificant, slow, old, uncoordinated.

Still, I hook my wagon to their rising star. Why? Because it separates me from the plebeians. It momentarily elevates me, knights me.

That philosophy motivated my fourth-grade friend Thomas to keep Dean Martin's cigarette butt in a jar next to his bedside. Dean Martin crooned his way into the heart of 1960s America via television, radio, and nightclubs. He shared thin-air celebrity status with Frank Sinatra and Sammy Davis Jr. We lowborns could only admire such nobility from a distance. Thomas, however, could do more. When Dean Martin graced our West Texas town by appearing in a charity golf tournament, Thomas and his father followed him in the gallery. When the icon flicked his cigarette to the side, Thomas was there to snag it.

Who could forget the moment when we,

the friends of Thomas, gathered in his bedroom to behold the holy stogie? We cashed in on the trickle-down principle of celebrity economy. Dean Martin was a star; Thomas owned Dean Martin's cigarette; we knew Thomas. We were down-the-line beneficiaries of Dean Martin's stardom.

Connect to someone special and become someone special, right?

Or simply outlive life. When the billionaire realizes that he will run out of years before he runs out of money, he establishes a foundation. No doubt some altruism motivates the move, but so does a hunger to matter.

We have kids for the same reason. Giving birth gives meaning to ourselves. Although parenthood is certainly a more noble reach for significance than showcasing Dean Martin's cigarette butt, it is still, in part, just that. One day, when we die, our descendants will remember "good ol' Dad" or "sweet ol' Mom," and we will extend our lives via theirs.

Italian jeans. Dean Martin's cigarette butt. Foundations. Legacies. Forever looking to prove Bertrand Russell wrong. He was the fatalistic atheist who concluded, "I believe that when I die my bones will rot and nothing shall remain of my ego."[1]

"He can't be right," we sigh.

"He isn't right!" Jesus announces. And in some of the kindest words ever heard, he allays the fear of the Stiltsvillians. "Are not two sparrows sold for a penny? Yet not one of them will fall to the ground apart from the will of your Father. And even the very hairs of your head are all numbered. So don't be afraid; you are worth more than many sparrows" (Matt. 10:29–31 NIV).

What's more inglorious than hair? Who inventories follicles? We monitor other resources: the amount of money in the bank, gas in the tank, pounds on the scale. But hair on the skin? No one, not even the man with the expanding bald spot, posts tiny number signs adjacent to each strand. We style hair, color hair, cut hair . . . but we don't count hair.

God does. "The very hairs of your head are all numbered."

So are the sparrows in the field. In the days of Jesus a penny was one of the smallest coins in circulation. One such penny would buy two sparrows. In other words, everyone could own a couple of sparrows. But why would they? What purpose did they serve? What goal would they accomplish?

In Luke's gospel Jesus goes a tender step further. "Are not five sparrows sold for two pennies? And not one of them is forgotten before God" (12:6 RSV). One penny would buy you two sparrows. Two pennies, however, would buy you five. The seller threw in the fifth for free.

Society still has its share of fifth sparrows: indistinct souls who feel dispensable, disposable, worth less than a penny. They drive carpools and work in cubicles. Some sleep beneath cardboard on the sidewalks and others beneath comforters in the suburbs. What they share is a feeling of smallness.

You'll find a flock of fifth sparrows in a Chinese orphanage for the deaf and mute. China's one-child policy has a way of weeding out the weak. Males are selected over females. Healthy babies outrank the impaired. Chinese children who cannot speak or hear stand little chance of a healthy, productive life. Every message tells them, "You don't matter."

So when someone says otherwise, they melt. Chinese missionary John Bentley describes such a moment. Deaf orphans in Henan province were given a Mandarin translation of a children's book I wrote entitled *You Are Special.* The story describes Punchinello, a wooden person in a village of wooden people. The villagers had a practice of sticking stars on the achievers and dots on the strugglers. Punchinello had so many dots that people gave him more dots for no reason at all.

But then he met Eli, his maker. Eli affirmed him, telling him to disregard the opinion of others. "I made you," he explained. "I don't make mistakes."

Punchinello had never heard such words. When he did, his dots began to fall off. And when the children in the Chinese orphanage heard such words, their worlds began to change. I'll let John describe the moment.

When they first distributed these books to the children and staff of the deaf school, the most bizarre thing happened. At a certain point everyone started crying. I could not understand this reaction. . . . Americans are somewhat used to the idea of positive reinforcement. . . . Not so in China and particularly not for these children who are virtually abandoned and considered valueless by their natural parents because they were born "broken." When the idea came through in the reading that they are special simply because they were made by a loving creator . . . everyone started crying — including their teachers! It was wild.[2]

Do you need this reminder? Any chance that these words are falling on the ears of a fifth sparrow? If so, it's time to deal with the fear of not mattering. Take this one seriously. The fear that you are one big zero will become a self-fulfilling prophecy that will ruin your life. It works like this.

You're slugging away at a menial job that pays poorly and saps your energy. The salary covers the bills but nothing more. Your God-given abilities languish like unwatered roses. But then you read of a job opening that capitalizes on your skills, maximizes your abilities. So in a moment of uncharacteristic courage, you submit your application. The employer invites you in for an interview. That's when the mentality of the Tribe of the Too Smalls returns. "I'll never impress them," you moan. "I'll look stupid in the interview. They'll ask questions I can't answer. I'll never get this job." A mouse in a lions' den has better odds of success. You flop miserably and descend yet another level into the basement of self-defeat.

Or consider the girl who is asked out on a date by a good-looking guy. So good-looking that she wonders what he sees in her. He's out of her league. Once he gets to know her, he'll drop her. Why, she may not be able to maintain his interest for one evening. Insecurity drives her to use the only tool she trusts, her body. She sleeps with him on the first date for fear that there won't be a second. She ends up feeling like the disposable woman she didn't want to become.

Fear of insignificance creates the result it dreads, arrives at the destination it tries to avoid, facilitates the scenario it disdains. If a basketball player stands at the foul line repeating, "I'll never make the shot, I'll never make the shot," guess what? He'll never make the shot. If you pass your days mumbling, "I'll never make a difference; I'm not worth anything," guess what? You will be sentencing yourself to a life of gloom without parole.

Even more, you are disagreeing with God. Questioning his judgment. Second-guessing his taste. According to him you were "skillfully wrought" (Ps. 139:15). You were "fearfully and wonderfully made" (Ps. 139:14). He can't stop thinking about you! If you could count his thoughts of you, "they would be more in number than the sand" (Ps. 139:18).

Why does he love you so much? The same reason the artist loves his paintings or the boat builder loves his vessels. You are his idea. And God has only good ideas. "For we are God's masterpiece. He has created us anew in Christ Jesus, so we can do the good things he planned for us long ago" (Eph. 2:10 NLT).

Every year tens of thousands of women attend the Women of Faith conferences. One reason they do is to hear words of comfort. After hearing one speaker after another describe God's compassion for each of his children, an attendee sent this e-mail.

In the movie *Hook,* Peter Pan had grown up, become old and overweight, and looked nothing like the Peter the lost boys knew. In the midst of the boys shouting that this was NOT Peter, one of the smallest boys took him by the hand and pulled him down to his level. He then placed his hands on Peter's face and proceeded to move the skin around, reshaping his face. The boy looked into Peter's eyes and said, "There you are, Peter!"

I brought a lot with me to Women of Faith, things that only God could see. But throughout the weekend I could feel God's hands on my face, pushing away all of the "stuff" I had brought. And then I could hear Him say, "There you are. There you are!"[3]

Shhh. Listen. Do you hear? God is saying the same words to you. Finding the beauty the years bury, the sparkle that time tries to take. Seeing you and loving the you he sees. "There you are. There you are."

He's enough. Isn't he? No more stilts or struts, spills or falls. Let others play the silly games. Not us. We've found something better. So, I'm told, have some of the people of Stiltsville.

Stiltsvillians still cluster,
and crowds still clamor,
but more stay away.
They seem less enamored

since the Carpenter came
and refused to be stilted.
He chose low over high,
left the system tip-tilted.

"You matter already,"
he explained to the town.
"Trust me on this one.
Keep your feet on the ground."

■ ■ ■ ■

CHAPTER 3
GOD'S TICKED
OFF AT ME

■ ■ ■ ■

Take courage, son; your sins are forgiven.
— MATTHEW 9:2 NASB

FEAR OF
DISAPPOINTING GOD

Noble Doss dropped the ball. One ball. One pass. One mistake. In 1941 he let one fall. And it's haunted him ever since. "I cost us a national championship," he says.

The University of Texas football team was ranked number one in the nation. Hoping for an undefeated season and a berth in the Rose Bowl, they played conference rival Baylor University. With a 7–0 lead in the third quarter, the Longhorn quarterback launched a deep pass to a wide-open Doss.

"The only thing I had between me and the goal," he recalls, "was twenty yards of grass."

The throw was on target. Longhorn fans rose to their feet. The sure-handed Doss spotted the ball and reached out, but it slipped through.

Baylor rallied and tied the score with seconds to play. Texas lost their top ranking

51

and, consequently, their chance at the Rose Bowl.

"I think about that play every day," Doss admits.

Not that he lacks other memories. Happily married for more than six decades. A father. Grandfather. He served in the navy during World War II. He appeared on the cover of *Life* magazine with his Texas teammates. He intercepted seventeen passes during his collegiate career, a university record. He won two NFL titles with the Philadelphia Eagles. The Texas High School Football Hall of Fame and the Longhorn Hall of Honor include his name.

Most fans remember the plays Doss made and the passes he caught. Doss remembers the one he missed. Once, upon meeting a new Longhorn head coach, Doss told him about the bobbled ball. It had been fifty years since the game, but he wept as he spoke.[1]

Memories of dropped passes fade slowly. They stir a lonely fear, a fear that we have disappointed people, that we have let down the team, that we've come up short. A fear that, when needed, we didn't do our part, that others suffered from our fumbles and bumbles. Of course, some of us would gladly swap our blunders for Doss's. If only we'd merely dropped a pass. If only we'd merely disappointed a football squad.

I converse often with a fellow who, by his own admission, wasted the first half of his life. Blessed with more talent than common sense, he made enemies and money at breakneck speed. Now he's the stuff of which sad country songs are written. Ruined marriage. Angry kids. His liver functions as if it's been soaked in vodka. (It has.)

When we talk, his eyes dart back and forth like a man hearing footsteps. His past pursues him like a posse. Our conversations return to the same orbit: "Can God ever forgive me?" "He gave me a wife; I blew it. He gave me kids; I blew it." I try to tell him, "Yes, you failed, but you aren't a failure. God came for people like us." He absorbs my words the way the desert absorbs a downpour. But by the next time I see him, he needs to hear them again. The parched soil of fear needs steady rain.

I correspond with a prisoner. Actually, he does most of the corresponding. He has three to five years to reflect on his financial misdealing. Shame and worry take turns dominating the pages — shame for the mistake, worry about the consequences. He's disappointed everyone he loves. Including God. Especially God. He fears he's outsinned God's patience.

He's not unique. "God's well of grace must have a bottom to it," we reason. "A person can request forgiveness only so many times," contends our common sense. "Cash in too many mercy checks, and sooner or later one is going to bounce!" The devil loves this line of logic. If he can convince us that God's grace has limited funds, we'll draw the logical conclusion. The account is empty. God has locked the door to his throne room. Pound all you want; pray all you want. No access to God.

"No access to God" unleashes a beehive of concerns. We are orphans, unprotected and exposed. Heaven, if there is such a place, has been removed from the itinerary. Vulnerable in this life and doomed in the next. The fear of disappointing God has teeth.

But Christ has forceps. In his first reference to fear, he does some serious defanging. "Take courage, son; your sins are forgiven" (Matt. 9:2 NASB). Note how Jesus places *courage* and *forgiven sins* in the same sentence. Might bravery begin when the problem of sin is solved? Let's see.

Jesus spoke these words to a person who could not move. "A paralytic lying on a bed . . ." (v. 2 NASB). The disabled man couldn't walk the dog or jog the neighborhood. But he did have four friends, and his friends had a hunch. When they got wind that Jesus was a guest in their town, they loaded their companion on a mat and went to see the teacher. An audience with Christ might bode well for their buddy.

A standing-room-only crowd packed the residence where Jesus spoke. People sat in windows, crowded in doorways. You'd have thought God himself was making the Capernaum appearance. Being the sort of fellows who don't give up easily, the friends concocted a plan. "When they weren't able to get in because of the crowd, they removed part of the roof and lowered the paraplegic on his stretcher" (Mark 2:4 MSG).

Risky strategy. Most home owners don't like to have their roofs disassembled. Most paraplegics aren't fond of a one-way bungee drop through a ceiling cavity. And most teachers don't appreciate a spectacle in the midst of their lesson. We don't know the reaction of the home owner or the man on the mat. But we know that Jesus didn't object. Matthew all but paints a smile on his face. Christ issued a blessing before one was requested. And he issued a blessing no one expected: "Take courage, son; your sins are forgiven" (Matt. 9:2 NASB). Wouldn't we anticipate different words? "Take courage. Your legs are healed." "Your paralysis is over." "Sign up for the Boston Marathon."

The man had limbs as sturdy as spaghetti, yet Jesus offered mercy, not muscles. What was he thinking? Simple. He was thinking about our deepest problem: sin. He was considering our deepest fear: the fear of failing God. Before Jesus healed the body (which he did), he treated the soul. "Take courage, son; your sins are forgiven."

To sin is to disregard God, ignore his teachings, deny his blessings. Sin is "Godless" living, centering life on the center letter of the word *sin*. The sinner's life is me-focused, not God-focused. Wasn't this the choice of Adam and Eve?

Prior to their sin they indwelled a fearless world. One with creation, one with God, one with each other. Eden was a "one-derful" world with one command: don't touch the tree of knowledge. Adam and Eve were given a choice, and each day they chose to trust God. But then came the serpent, sowing seeds of doubt and offering a sweeter deal. "Has God indeed said . . . ," he questioned (Gen. 3:1). "You will be like God," he offered (Gen. 3:5).

Just like that, Eve was afraid. Some say she was pride filled, defiant, disobedient . . .

56

but wasn't she first afraid? Afraid that God was holding out, that she was missing out? Afraid Eden wasn't enough? Afraid God wasn't enough? Afraid God couldn't deliver?

Suppose she and Adam had defied these fears. Refused to give soil to the serpent's seeds of doubt. "You're wrong, you reptile. Our Maker has provided for each and every need. We have no reason to doubt him. Go back to the hole from which you came." But they spoke no such words. They mishandled fear, and fear did them in.

Eve quit trusting God and took matters — and the fruit — into her own hands. "Just in case God can't do it, I will." Adam followed suit.

Adam and Eve did what fear-filled people do. They ran for their lives. "Adam and his wife hid themselves from the presence of the LORD God among the trees of the garden. Then the LORD God called to Adam and said to him, 'Where are you?' So he said, 'I heard Your voice in the garden, and I was afraid' " (Gen. 3:8–10).

Fear, mismanaged, leads to sin. Sin leads to hiding. Since we've all sinned, we all hide, not in bushes, but in eighty-hour workweeks, temper tantrums, and religious busyness. We avoid contact with God.

We are convinced that God must hate our

evil tendencies. We sure do. We don't like the things we do and say. We despise our lustful thoughts, harsh judgments, and self-ish deeds. If our sin nauseates us, how much more must it revolt a holy God! We draw a practical conclusion: God is irreparably ticked off at us. So what are we to do except duck into the bushes at the sound of his voice?

The prophet Isaiah says that sin has left us as lost and confused as stray sheep. "All we like sheep have gone astray; we have turned, every one, to his own way" (Isa. 53:6). If the prophet had known my dog, he might have written, "All we like Molly have gone astray . . ."

For such a sweet dog, she has a stubborn, defiant streak. Once her nose gets wind of a neighbor's grilling steak or uncovered trash, no amount of commands can control her. You don't want to know how many times this minister has chased his dog down the street, tossing un-minister-like warnings at his pet. She "sins," living as if her master doesn't exist. She is known to wander.

Last week we thought she'd wandered away for good. We posted her picture on bulletin boards, drove through the neighbor-hood, calling her name. Finally, after a day of futility, I went to the animal shelter. I described Molly to the animal shelter director. She wished me luck and pointed toward a barrack-shaped building whose door bore the sign Stray Dogs.

Warning to softhearted dog lovers: don't go there! I've not seen such sadness since they shut down the drive-in movie theater in my hometown. Cage after cage of longing, frightened eyes. Big, round ones. Narrow, dark ones. Some peered from beneath the thick eyebrows of a cocker spaniel. Others from the bald-as-a-rock head of a Chihuahua. Different breeds but same plight. Lost as blind geese with no clue how to get home.

Two terriers, according to a note on the gate, were found on a remote highway. Someone found an aging poodle in an alley. I thought I'd found her when I spotted a golden retriever with salty hair. But it wasn't Molly. It was a he with eyes so brown and lonely they nearly landed him a place in my backseat.

I didn't find Molly at the shelter.

I did have a crazy urge at the shelter, however. I wanted to announce Jesus' declaration: "Be of good cheer. You are lost no more!" I wanted to take the strays home with me, to unlock door after door and fill my car with barking, tail-wagging *dog*igals.

I didn't do it. As much as I wanted to save the dogs, I wanted to stay married even more.

But I did have the urge, and the urge helps me understand why Jesus made forgiveness his first fearless announcement. Yes, we have disappointed God. But, no, God has not abandoned us.

[We are] delivered . . . from the power of darkness and conveyed . . . into the kingdom of the Son. (Col. 1:13)

He who believes in Him is not condemned. (John 3:18)

Everyone who looks to the Son and believes in him shall have eternal life, and I will raise him up at the last day. (John 6:40 NIV)

These things I have written to you who believe in the name of the Son of God, that you may *know* that you have eternal life. (1 John 5:13)

Jesus loves us too much to leave us in doubt about his grace. His "perfect love expels all fear" (1 John 4:18 NLT). If God loved with an imperfect love, we would have high cause to worry. Imperfect love keeps a list of sins and consults it often. God keeps no list of our wrongs. His love casts out fear because he casts out our sin!

Tether your heart to this promise, and tighten the knot. Remember the words of John's epistle: "If our heart condemns us, God is greater than our heart, and knows all things" (1 John 3:20). When you feel unforgiven, evict the feelings. Emotions don't get a vote. Go back to Scripture. God's Word holds rank over self-criticism and self-doubt.

As Paul told Titus, "God's readiness to give and forgive is now public. Salvation's available for everyone! . . . Tell them all this. Build up their *courage*" (Titus 2:11, 15 MSG). Do you know God's grace? Then you can love boldly, live robustly. You can swing from trapeze to trapeze; his safety net will break your fall.

Nothing fosters courage like a clear grasp of grace.

And nothing fosters fear like an ignorance of mercy. May I speak candidly? If you haven't accepted God's forgiveness, you are doomed to fear. Nothing can deliver you from the gnawing realization that you have disregarded your Maker and disobeyed his instruction. No pill, pep talk, psychiatrist, or possession can set the sinner's heart at ease. You may deaden the fear, but you can't remove it. Only God's grace can.

Have you accepted the forgiveness of Christ? If not, do so. "If we confess our sins, He is faithful and just to forgive us our sins and to cleanse us from all unrighteousness" (1 John 1:9). Your prayer can be as simple as this: *Dear Father, I need forgiveness. I admit that I have turned away from you. Please forgive me. I place my soul in your hands and my trust in your grace. Through Jesus I pray, amen.*

Having received God's forgiveness, live forgiven! Jesus has healed your legs, so walk. Jesus has opened the cage of the kennel, so step out. When Jesus sets you free, you are free indeed.

But you may need to silence some roosters. Booker T. Washington relates a helpful story of the day his mother did so. Every morning of his young life, he, along with all the plantation slaves, was awakened by the crow of a rooster. Long before daybreak the unwelcome noise would fill the sod shanties, reminding Washington and his fellow workers to crawl out of bed and leave for the cotton fields. The rooster's crow came to symbolize their dictated life of long days and backbreaking labor.

But then came the Emancipation Proclamation. Abraham Lincoln pronounced freedom for slaves. The first morning afterward, young Booker was awakened by the rooster again. Only this time his mother was chasing it around the barnyard with an ax. The Washington family fried and ate their alarm clock for lunch. Their first act of freedom was to silence the reminder of slavery.

Any roosters stealing your sleep? You might need to sharpen the blade. The great news of the gospel is, yes, his grace is real, and so is our freedom.[2]

By the way, the case of the missing Molly? She turned up in a neighbor's backyard. Turns out she wasn't as far from home as we all feared. Neither are you.

■ ■ ■ ■

CHAPTER 4
WOE, BE GONE

■ ■ ■ ■

I tell you not to worry about everyday life
— whether you have enough.
— MATTHEW 6:25 NLT

FEAR OF RUNNING OUT

Worry stands in the airport security line and removes her bracelet. She's already placed her shoes in a rubberized bin and liquids in the plastic bag and has removed the boarding pass from her purse. Her stomach tightens as she awaits her turn to step through the body scanner that will identify her as weaponless. Worry wonders about the fungus on the floor, the skill of the screeners, and what happened to the day when a traveler could walk straight to the gate and catch the flight. She hates the thought but permits it anyway. *Any day now our luck is going to run out.* She looks beyond the X-ray machine to the TSA agent, who runs a wand around the body of a grandmother. Worry starts to feel sorry for her, then decides not to. Terrorists grow old too. She worries that the grandmother is on her flight.

Worry sits on the back row of the English

as a Second Language class. He'd prefer the front row, but by the time he caught the city bus and endured the evening traffic, the best seats were taken. His hands still smell of diner dishwater where Worry worked since six this morning. Within twelve hours he'll be at the sink again, but for now he does his best to make sense of verbs, adverbs, and nouns. Everyone else seems to get it. He doesn't. He never diagrammed a sentence in Spanish; how will he ever do it in English? Yet with no English how will he ever do more than wash plates? Worry has more questions than answers, more work than energy, and thinks often about giving up.

Worry thinks her son should wear a scarf. Today's temperature won't warm beyond freezing, and she knows he will spend the better part of his lunch hour kicking a soccer ball over the frozen grass. She knows better than to tell him to wear it. Thirteen-year-olds don't wear scarves. But her thirteen-year-old is prone to throat infections and earaches, so she shoves a wrap into his backpack next to the algebra homework that kept them both up past bedtime last night. Worry reminds him to review the assignment, gives him a kiss, and watches him run out the door to board the awaiting bus. She looks up at the gray sky and asks God if he ever air-drops relief packages to weary moms. "You have one needing some strength down here."

Worry awoke at 4:30 a.m. today, struggling with this chapter. It needs to be finished by 5:00 p.m. I pulled the pillow over my head and tried in vain to return to the blissful netherworld of sleep that knows nothing of deadlines or completion dates. But it was too late. The starter's pistol had fired. An Olympic squad of synapses was racing in my brain, stirring a wake of adrenaline. So Worry climbed out of bed, dressed, and slipped out of the house into the silent streets and drove to the office. I grumbled, first about the crowded calendar, next about my poor time management. Worry unlocked the door, turned on the computer, stared at the passage on the monitor, and smiled at the first verse: Jesus' definition of worry.

That is why I tell you not to worry about everyday life — whether you have enough. (Matt. 6:25 NLT)

Whether you have enough. Shortfalls and depletions inhabit our trails. Not enough time, luck, credit, wisdom, intelligence. We are running out of everything, it seems, and so we worry. But worry doesn't work.

> Look at the birds. They don't plant or harvest or store food in barns, for your heavenly Father feeds them. And aren't you far more valuable to him than they are? Can all your worries add a single moment to your life? (vv. 26–27 NLT)

Fret won't fill a bird's belly with food or a flower's petal with color. Birds and flowers seem to get along just fine, and they don't take antacids. What's more, you can dedicate a decade of anxious thoughts to the brevity of life and not extend it by one minute. Worry accomplishes nothing.

Suppose I had responded differently to the uninvited wake-up call. Rather than tackle the task, suppose I had curled up in a fetal position and bemoaned my pathetic state. "The publisher expects too much! Every year another book. Every book complete with chapters. Why, not even Jesus could bear up under such stress. I'll never meet the deadline. When I don't, the editorial staff will hate me and revoke my contract. Bookstores will learn of my missed deadline and will burn Lucado books in their parking lots. My wife will be humiliated, my children ostracized. I think I'll have Jack Daniel's for breakfast."

See what happened? Legitimate concern morphed into toxic panic. I crossed a boundary line into the state of fret. No longer anticipating or preparing, I took up membership in the fraternity of Woe-Be-Me. Christ cautions us against this. Look at how one translation renders his words: "Therefore I tell you, stop being perpetually uneasy (anxious and worried) about your life" (Matt. 6:25 AMP).

Jesus doesn't condemn legitimate concern for responsibilities but rather the continuous mind-set that dismisses God's presence. Destructive anxiety subtracts God from the future, faces uncertainties with no faith, tallies up the challenges of the day without entering God into the equation. Worry is the darkroom where negatives become glossy prints.

A friend saw an example of perpetual uneasiness in his six-year-old daughter. In her hurry to dress for school, she tied her shoelaces in a knot. She plopped down at the base of the stairs and lasered her thoughts on the tangled mess. The school bus was coming, and the minutes were ticking, and she gave no thought to the fact that

71

her father was standing nearby, willing to help upon request. Her little hands began to shake, and tears began to drop. Finally, in an expression of total frustration, she dropped her forehead to her knees and sobbed.

That's a child-sized portrait of destructive worry. A knot fixation to the point of anger and exasperation, oblivious to the presence of our Father, who stands nearby. My friend finally took it upon himself to come to his daughter's aid.

Why didn't she request her father's help to start with? We could ask the same question of the disciples. They were one request away from help.

Jesus had taken them on a retreat. His heart was heavied by the news of the murder of John the Baptist, so he told his disciples, "Come aside by yourselves to a deserted place and rest a while" (Mark 6:31).

But then came the hungry crowd. Droves of people — fifteen, maybe twenty, thousand individuals — followed them. A multitude of misery and sickness who brought nothing but needs. Jesus treated the people with kindness. The disciples didn't share his compassion. "That evening the disciples came to him and said, 'This is a remote place, and it's already getting late. Send the crowds away so they can go to the villages and buy food for themselves' " (Matt. 14:15 NLT).

Whoops, somebody was a bit testy. The followers typically prefaced their comments with the respectful *Lord.* Not this time. Anxiety makes tyrants out of us. They issued a command, not a request: "Send them home so they can buy food for themselves." *Do they think we have the keys to Fort Knox?* The disciples didn't have the resources for such a mob.

Their disrespect didn't perturb Jesus; he simply issued them an assignment: "They do not need to go away. You give them something to eat" (v. 16). I'm imagining a few shoulder shrugs and rolled eyes, the disciples huddling and tallying their supplies. Peter likely led the discussion with a bark: "Let's count the bread: one, two, three, four, five. I have five loaves. Andrew, you check me on this." He does: "One, two, three, four, five . . ."

Peter set aside the bread and inquired about the fish. Same routine, lower number. "Fish? Let me see. One, two, three . . . Change that. I counted one fish twice. Looks like the grand total of fish is two!"

The aggregate was declared. "We have here only five loaves and two fish" (v. 17).

The descriptor *only* stands out. As if to say, "Our resources are hopelessly puny. There is nothing left but this wimpy lunch." The fuel needle was on empty; the clock was on the last hour; the pantry was down to crumbs. Philip added a personal audit: "Eight months' wages would not buy enough bread for each one to have a bite!" (John 6:7 NIV). The exclamation point was an exasperation point. "Your assignment is too great!"

How do you suppose Jesus felt about the basket inventory? Any chance he might have wanted them to include the rest of the possibilities? Involve all the options? Do you think he was hoping someone might count to eight?

"Well, let's see. We have five loaves, two fish, and . . . Jesus!" Jesus Christ. The same Jesus who told us:

> Ask and it will be given to you; seek and you will find; knock and the door will be opened to you. (Luke 11:9 NIV)

> If you remain in me and my words remain in you, ask whatever you wish, and it will be given you. (John 15:7 NIV)

> Whatever you ask for in prayer, believe

that you have received it, and it will be yours. (Mark 11:24 NIV)

Standing next to the disciples was the solution to their problems . . . but they didn't go to him. They stopped their count at seven and worried.

What about you? Are you counting to seven, or to eight?

Here are eight worry-stoppers to expand your tally:

1. *Pray, first.* Don't pace up and down the floors of the waiting room; pray for a successful surgery. Don't bemoan the collapse of an investment; ask God to help you. Don't join the chorus of co-workers who complain about your boss; invite them to bow their heads with you and pray for him. Inoculate yourself inwardly to face your fears outwardly. "Casting the whole of your care [all your anxieties, all your worries, all your concerns, once and for all] on Him . . ." (1 Peter 5:7 AMP).

2. *Easy, now.* Slow down. "Rest in the LORD, and wait patiently for Him" (Ps. 37:7). Imitate the mother of Jesus at the wedding in Cana. The reception was out of wine, a huge social no-no in the days of Jesus. Mary could have blamed the host for poor planning or the guests for overdrink-

ing, but she didn't catastrophize. No therapy sessions or counseling. Instead, she took the shortage straight to Jesus. "When they ran out of wine, the mother of Jesus said to Him, 'They have no wine' " (John 2:3). See how quickly you can do the same. Assess the problem. Take it to Jesus and state it clearly.

3. *Act on it.* Become a worry-slapper. Treat frets like mosquitoes. Do you procrastinate when a bloodsucking bug lights on your skin? "I'll take care of it in a moment." Of course you don't! You give the critter the slap it deserves. Be equally decisive with anxiety. The moment a concern surfaces, deal with it. Don't dwell on it. Head off worries before they get the best of you. Don't waste an hour wondering what your boss thinks; ask her. Before you diagnose that mole as cancer, have it examined. Instead of assuming you'll never get out of debt, consult an expert. Be a doer, not a stewer.

4. *Compile a worry list.* Over a period of days record your anxious thoughts. Maintain a list of all the things that trouble you. Then review them. How many of them turned into a reality? You worried that the house would burn down. Did it? That your job would be outsourced. Was it?

5. *Evaluate your worry categories.* Your list will highlight themes of worry. You'll detect recurring areas of preoccupation that may become obsessions: what people think of you, finances, global calamities, your appearance or performance. Pray specifically about them.

6. *Focus on today.* God meets daily needs daily. Not weekly or annually. He will give you what you need when it is needed. "Let us therefore boldly approach the throne of our gracious God, where we may receive mercy and in his grace find *timely* help" (Heb. 4:16 NEB). An ancient hymn expresses the heart this patient waiting creates.

Not so in haste, my heart!
Have faith in God, and wait;
Although He linger long,
He never comes too late.

He never comes too late;
He knoweth what is best;
Vex not thyself in vain;
Until He cometh, rest.

Until He cometh, rest,
Nor grudge the hours that roll;
The feet that wait for God

Are soonest at the goal.

Are soonest at the goal
That is not gained with speed;
Then hold thee still, my heart,
For I shall wait His lead.[1]

7. *Unleash a worry army.* Share your feelings with a few loved ones. Ask them to pray with and for you. They're more willing to help than you might imagine. Less worry on your part means more happiness on theirs.

8. *Let God be enough.* Jesus concludes his call to calmness with this challenge: "Your heavenly Father already knows all your needs. Seek the Kingdom of God above all else, and live righteously, and he will give you everything you need" (Matt. 6:32–33 NLT).

Seek first the kingdom of wealth, and you'll worry over every dollar. Seek first the kingdom of health, and you'll sweat every blemish and bump. Seek first the kingdom of popularity, and you'll relive every conflict. Seek first the kingdom of safety, and you'll jump at every crack of the twig. But seek first his kingdom, and you will find it. On that, we can depend and never worry.

Eight steps. **P**ray, first. **E**asy, now. **A**ct on it. **C**ompile a worry list. **E**valuate your worry categories. **F**ocus on today. **U**nleash a worry army. **L**et God be enough.

P-E-A-C-E-F-U-L.

(I'd better stop with that. It's nearly 5:00 p.m.)

■ ■ ■ ■

CHAPTER 5
MY CHILD IS
IN DANGER

■ ■ ■ ■

Don't be afraid. Just believe, and your
daughter will be well.
— LUKE 8:50 NCV

FEAR OF NOT PROTECTING MY KIDS

No one told me that newborns make night-time noises. All night long. They gurgle; they pant. They whimper; they whine. They smack their lips and sigh. They keep Daddy awake. At least Jenna kept me awake. I wanted Denalyn to sleep. Thanks to a medication mix-up, her post-C-section rest was scant. So for our first night home with our first child, I volunteered to serve as first responder. We wrapped our eight pounds and four ounces of beauty in a soft pink blanket, placed her in the bassinet, and set it next to my side of the bed. Denalyn fell quickly into a sound slumber. Jenna followed her mom's example. And Dad? This dad didn't know what to make of the baby noises.

When Jenna's breathing slowed, I leaned my ear onto her mouth to see if she was alive. When her breathing hurried, I looked up "infant hyperventilation" in the family medical encyclopedia. When she burbled and panted, so did I. After a couple of hours I realized, *I have no clue how to behave!* I lifted Jenna out of her bed, carried her into the living room of our apartment, and sat in a rocker. That's when a tsunami of sobriety washed over me.

"We're in charge of a human being."

I don't care how tough you are. You may be a Navy SEAL who specializes in high-altitude skydiving behind enemy lines. You might spend each day making million-dollar, split-second stock market decisions. Doesn't matter. Every parent melts the moment he or she feels the full force of parenthood.

I did.

How did I get myself into this? I retraced my steps. First came love, then came marriage, then the *discussions* of a baby carriage. Of course I was open to the idea. Especially when I considered my role in launching the effort. Somehow during the nine-month expansion project, the reality of fatherhood didn't dawn on me. Women are nodding and smiling. "Never underestimate the density of a man," you say. True. But moms have an advantage: thirty-six weeks of reminders elbowing around inside them. Our kick in the gut comes later. But it does come. And for me it came in the midnight quiet of an apartment living room in downtown Rio de Janeiro, Brazil, as I held a human being in my arms.

The semitruck of parenting comes loaded with fears. We fear failing the child, forgetting the child. Will we have enough money? Enough answers? Enough diapers? Enough drawer space? Vaccinations. Educations. Homework. Homecoming. It's enough to keep a parent awake at night.

And even though we learn to cope, an apiary of dangers buzzes in the background. Consider the mom who called me last evening. A custody battle rages around her ten-year-old son. The courts, the father, the mother, the lawyers — they're stretching the boy like taffy. She wonders if her child will survive the ordeal.

So do the parents of the teenage daughter who collapsed in a volleyball workout. No one knew about her heart condition or knows how she'll fare. When we prayed at her bedside, her mom's tears left circles on the sheets.

At least they know where their child is. The mother who called our church for prayers doesn't. Her daughter, a high school senior, ran away with a boyfriend. He's into drugs. She's into him. Both are into trouble.

85

The mother begs for help.

Fear distilleries concoct a high-octane brew for parents — a primal, gut-wrenching, pulse-stilling dose. Whether Mom and Dad keep vigil outside a neonatal unit, make weekly visits to a juvenile prison, or hear the crunch of a bike and the cry of a child in the driveway, their reaction is the same: "I have to do something." No parent can sit still while his or her child suffers.

Jairus couldn't.

> On the other side of the lake the crowds welcomed Jesus, because they had been waiting for him. Then a man named Jairus, a leader of the local synagogue, came and fell at Jesus' feet, pleading with him to come home with him. His only daughter, who was about twelve years old, was dying. As Jesus went with him, he was surrounded by the crowds. (Luke 8:40–42 NLT)

Jairus was a Capernaum community leader, "one of the rulers of the synagogue" (Mark 5:22). Mayor, bishop, and ombudsman, all in one. The kind of man a city would send to welcome a celebrity. But when Jairus approached Jesus on the Galilean shoreline, he wasn't representing his village; he was pleading on behalf of his child.

Urgency stripped the formalities from his greeting. He issued no salutation or compliment, just a prayer of panic. Another gospel reads: "[Jairus] fell at his feet, pleading fervently with him. 'My little daughter is dying,' he said. 'Please come and lay your hands on her; heal her so she can live' " (Mark 5:22–23 NLT).

Jairus isn't the only parent to run onto gospel pages on behalf of a child. A mother stormed out of the Canaanite hills, crying, "Mercy, Master, Son of David! My daughter is cruelly afflicted by an evil spirit" (Matt. 15:22 MSG). A father of a seizure-tormented boy sought help from the disciples, then Jesus. He cried out with tears, "Lord, I believe; help my unbelief!" (Mark 9:24).

The Canaanite mother. The father of the epileptic boy. Jairus. These three parents form an unwitting New Testament society: struggling parents of stricken children. They held the end of their rope in one hand and reached toward Christ with the other. In each case Jesus responded. He never turned one away.

His consistent kindness issues a welcome announcement: Jesus heeds the concern in the parent's heart.

After all, our kids were his kids first. "Don't you see that children are GOD'S best gift? the fruit of the womb his generous legacy?" (Ps. 127:3 MSG). Before they were ours, they were his. Even as they are ours, they are still his.

We tend to forget this fact, regarding our children as "our" children, as though we have the final say in their health and welfare. We don't. All people are God's people, including the small people who sit at our tables. Wise are the parents who regularly give their children back to God.

Abraham famously modeled this. The father of the faith was also the father of Isaac. Abraham and Sarah waited nearly a century for this child to be born. I don't know which is more amazing, that Sarah became pregnant at the age of ninety or that she and Abraham at that age were still trying to conceive. Of all the gifts God gave them, Isaac was the greatest. Of all the commands God gave Abraham, this one was the hardest: "He said, 'Take your dear son Isaac whom you love and go to the land of Moriah. Sacrifice him there as a burnt offering on one of the mountains that I'll point out to you' " (Gen. 22:2 MSG).

Abraham saddled the donkey, took Isaac and two servants, and traveled to the place of sacrifice. When he saw the mountain in the distance, he instructed the servants to stay and wait. And he made a statement that is worthy of special note: "Stay here with the donkey. My son and I will go over there and worship, and then we will come back to you" (Gen. 22:5 NCV).

Look at Abraham's confident "*we* will come back." "Abraham reasoned that if Isaac died, God was able to bring him back to life again. And in a sense, Abraham did receive his son back from the dead" (Heb. 11:19 NLT). God interrupted the sacrifice and spared Isaac.

Jairus was hoping for the same with his daughter. He begged Jesus to come to his home (Luke 8:41). The father wasn't content with long-distance assistance; he wanted Christ beneath his roof, walking through his rooms, standing at the bedside of his daughter. He wanted the presence of Christ to permeate his house.

My wife displays this same longing. I will someday ask God, "Why were you so good to my daughters and me?" and he will answer by pointing to Denalyn. "She just kept talking about you and your kids." Denalyn takes regular prayer walks through our house, stepping into each bedroom and living area. She pauses to pray for her daughters and husband. She takes full advantage of the invitation of Lamentations 2:19: "Pour out your heart like water before the face of the Lord. Lift your hands toward Him for the life of your young children" (Lam. 2:19).

Parents, we can do this. We can be loyal advocates, stubborn intercessors. We can take our parenting fears to Christ. In fact, if we don't, we'll take our fears out on our kids. Fear turns some parents into paranoid prison guards who monitor every minute, check the background of every friend. They stifle growth and communicate distrust. A family with no breathing room suffocates a child.

On the other hand, fear can also create permissive parents. For fear that their child will feel too confined or fenced in, they lower all boundaries. High on hugs and low on discipline. They don't realize that appropriate discipline is an expression of love. Permissive parents. Paranoid parents. How can we avoid the extremes? We pray.

Prayer is the saucer into which parental fears are poured to cool. Jesus says so little about parenting, makes no comments about spanking, breast-feeding, sibling rivalry, or schooling. Yet his actions speak volumes about prayer. Each time a parent prays,

Christ responds. His big message to moms and dads? Bring your children to me. Raise them in a greenhouse of prayer.

When you send them off for the day, do so with a blessing. When you tell them good night, cover them in prayer. Is your daughter stumped by geography homework? Pray with her about it. Is your son intimidated by the new girl? Pray with him about her. Pray that your children have a profound sense of place in this world and a heavenly place in the next.

Some years ago I witnessed a father taking this priority seriously during a Sunday morning worship service. As we took communion, I heard a small boy asking, "What's that, Daddy?" The father explained the meaning of the bread and then offered a prayer. The boy was quiet until the cup was passed. Then he asked again, "What's that, Daddy?" The father began again, explaining the blood and the cross and how the wine symbolizes Jesus' death. Then he prayed.

I chuckled at the colossal task the father was tackling. When I turned to give him a knowing nod, I realized the father was David Robinson, NBA basketball player for the San Antonio Spurs. Sitting on his lap was his six-year-old son, David Jr.

Less than twenty-four hours earlier David

had led the Spurs in scoring in a play-off game against the Phoenix Suns. Within twenty-four hours David would be back in Phoenix, doing the same. But sandwiched between the two nationally televised, high-stakes contests was David the dad. Not David the MVP or Olympic Gold Medal winner, but David the father, explaining holy communion to David the son.

Of the events of that weekend, which mattered most? The basketball games or the communion service? Which will have eternal consequences? The points scored on the court? Or the message shared at church? What will make the biggest difference in young David's life? Watching his dad play basketball or hearing him whisper a prayer?

Parents, we can't protect children from every threat in life, but we can take them to the Source of life. We can entrust our kids to Christ. Even then, however, our shoreline appeals may be followed by a difficult choice.

As Jairus and Jesus were going to Jairus's home, "a messenger arrived from the home of Jairus, the leader of the synagogue. He told him, 'Your daughter is dead. There's no use troubling the Teacher now.' But when Jesus heard what had happened, he said to Jairus, 'Don't be afraid. Just have faith, and she will be healed' " (Luke 8:49–50 NLT).

Jairus was whipsawed between the contrasting messages. The first, from the servants: "Your daughter is dead." The second, from Jesus: "Don't be afraid." Horror called from one side. Hope compelled from the other. Tragedy, then trust. Jairus heard two voices and had to choose which one he would heed.

Don't we all?

The hard reality of parenting reads something like this: you can do your best and still stand where Jairus stood. You can protect, pray, and keep all the bogeymen at bay and still find yourself in an ER at midnight or a drug rehab clinic on visitors' Sunday, choosing between two voices: despair and belief. Jairus could have chosen despair. Who would have faulted him for deciding "Enough is enough"? He had no guarantee that Jesus could help. His daughter was dead. Jairus could have walked away. As parents, we're so glad he didn't. We need to know what Jesus will do when we entrust our kids to him.

He *united the household.* "When Jesus went to the house, he let only Peter, John, James, and the girl's father and mother go inside with him" (Luke 8:51 NCV).

Jesus included the mother. Until this point

she had been, for whatever reason, out of the picture. Perhaps she was at her daughter's bedside. Or she might have been at odds with her husband. Crisis can divide a family. The stress of caring for a sick or troubled child can drive a wedge between Mom and Dad. But here, Christ united them. Picture Jesus pausing at the house entrance, gesturing for the distraught mother to join them. He didn't have to do so. He could have hurried in without her. But he wanted Mom and Dad to stand together in the struggle. Jesus gathered the entire, albeit small, household in the presence of the daughter.

And he *banished unbelief.* "Now all wept and mourned for her; but He said, 'Do not weep; she is not dead, but sleeping.' And they ridiculed Him, knowing that she was dead. But He put them all outside" (vv. 52–54).

He commanded doubt to depart and permitted only faith and hope to stay. And in this intimate circle of trust, Jesus "took her by the hand and called, saying, 'Little girl, arise.' Then her spirit returned, and she arose immediately. And He commanded that she be given something to eat. And her parents were astonished" (vv. 54–56).

God has a heart for hurting parents.

Should we be surprised? After all, God himself is a father. What parental emotion has he not felt? Are you separated from your child? So was God. Is someone mistreating your child? They mocked and bullied his. Is someone taking advantage of your children? The Son of God was set up by false testimony and betrayed by a greedy follower. Are you forced to watch while your child suffers? God watched his son on the cross. Do you find yourself wanting to spare your child from all the hurt in the world? God did. But because of his great love for us, "he did not spare his own Son but gave him for us all. So with Jesus, God will surely give us all things" (Rom. 8:32 NCV).

"All things" must include courage and hope.

Some of you find the story of Jairus difficult to hear. You prayed the same prayer he did, yet you found yourself in a cemetery facing every parent's darkest night: the death of your child. No pain compares. What hope does the story of Jairus offer to you? Jesus resurrected Jairus's child. Why didn't he save yours?

God understands your question. He buried a child too. He hates death more than you do. That's why he killed it. He "abolished death and brought life and immortality to light" (2 Tim. 1:10). For those who trust God, death is nothing more than a transition to heaven. Your child may not be in your arms, but your child is safely in his.

Others of you have been standing for a long time where Jairus stood. You've long since left the water's edge of offered prayer but haven't yet arrived at the household of answered prayer. You've wept a monsoon of tears for your child, enough to summon the attention of every angel and their neighbor to your cause. At times you've felt that a breakthrough was nearing, that Christ was following you to your house. But you're not so sure anymore. You find yourself alone on the path, wondering if Christ has forgotten you and your child.

He hasn't. He never dismisses a parent's prayer. Keep giving your child to God, and in the right time and the right way, God will give your child back to you.

Late that night a quarter century ago, I gave my daughter to God. As I rocked her in our just-bought rocker, I remembered the way Abraham had placed Isaac on the altar, and I decided to do the same. So following the centenarian's example, I made our apartment living room my Moriah and lifted my daughter toward heaven. *I can't raise this girl,* I confessed, *but you can. I give her back to you.* Must have been a sight to behold, a pajama-clad father lifting his blanket-wrapped baby toward the ceiling. But something tells me that a few parents appreciated the gesture. Among them, Abraham, Jairus, and, of course, God.

■ ■ ■ ■

CHAPTER 6
I'M SINKING FAST

■ ■ ■ ■

"Don't be afraid," he said. "Take courage.
I am here!"
— MATTHEW 14:27 NLT

FEAR OF
OVERWHELMING
CHALLENGES

Before the flight I'm a midlife version of Tom Cruise in *Top Gun:* wearing an air force helmet, a flight suit, and a smile the size of a watermelon slice. After the flight Top Gun is undone. I'm as pale as bleached bone. I list to the side, and my big smile has flattened as straight as the tarmac on which we just landed. Chalk the change up to sixty minutes of acrobatics at ten thousand feet.

I occupied the cockpit seat directly behind Lt. Col. Tom McClain. One month shy of retirement he invited me to join him on an orientation flight. The invitation came complete with

- a preflight physical (in which I was measured for the ejection seat);
- a safety briefing (in which I practiced pulling the handle for the ejection seat);
- a few moments hanging in the harness

of a training parachute (simulating how I would return to earth after any activation of the ejection seat).

Message to air force public relations: any way to scale down the ejection-seat discussion? Turns out we didn't use it. No small accomplishment since we dived, rose, and dived again, sometimes with a vertical velocity of ten thousand feet per minute. Can you picture a roller coaster minus the rails? We flew in tandem with another T-6. At one point the two wingtips were separated by seven feet. I don't like to get that close to another person in the shopping mall.

Here's what one hour of aerial somersaults taught me:

- Fighter pilots are underpaid. I have no clue what their salary is, but it's not enough. Anyone willing to protect his country at 600 mph deserves a bonus.
- G's are well named. Funny, I thought the phrase "pulling g's" had to do with gravitational pull against your body. It actually describes the involuntary sound a minister emits during a 360-degree rollover: "G-G-G-Geee!"
- The call sign of the pilot is stenciled on the back of his helmet.

102

They have such great call signs: Iceman. Buff. Hatchet. Mine was Max. Pretty cool, huh? Col. McClain responds to T-Mac. It appears on the back of his helmet just above the collar line. I know this well. For fifty of the sixty minutes, I stared at his name. I read it forward, then backward, counted the letters, and created an acrostic: T-M-A-C. **T**ell **M**e **A**bout **C**hrist. I couldn't stomach looking anywhere else. The horizon kept bouncing. So did the instrument panel. Closing my eyes only increased the nausea. So I stared at T-Mac. After all, he was the one with nearly six thousand hours of flight time!

Six thousand hours! He's spent more time flying planes than I've spent eating pizza, a thought that occurred to me as I began regretting my dinner from the night before. Six thousand hours! The equivalent of eight months' worth of twenty-four-hour days in the air, time enough to circumnavigate the globe 143 times. No wonder he was smiling when we boarded. This sortie was a bike ride on training wheels. I actually heard him humming during a near-vertical bank turn.

Didn't take me long to figure out where to stare. No more looking down or out. My eyes were on the pilot. If T-Mac was okay, I was okay. I know where to stare in turbulence.

Peter learned the same lesson the hard way. Exchange the plane for a thirty-foot fishing boat, the San Antonio sky for a Galilean sea, and our stories begin to parallel. "But the boat was now in the middle of the sea, tossed by the waves, for the wind was contrary" (Matt. 14:24).

As famous lakes go, Galilee — only thirteen miles at its longest, seven and a half at its widest — is a small, moody one. The diminutive size makes it more vulnerable to the winds that howl out of the Golan Heights. They turn the lake into a blender, shifting suddenly, blowing first from one direction, then another. Winter months bring such storms every two weeks or so, churning the waters for two to three days at a time.[1]

Peter and his fellow storm riders knew they were in trouble. What should have been a sixty-minute cruise became a nightlong battle. The boat lurched and lunged like a kite in a March wind. Sunlight was a distant memory. Rain fell from the night sky in buckets. Lightning sliced the blackness with a silver sword. Winds whipped the sails, leaving the disciples "in the middle of the sea, tossed by the waves." Apt description, perhaps, for your stage in life? Perhaps all we need to do is substitute a couple of nouns . . .

In the middle of a divorce, tossed about by guilt.

In the middle of debt, tossed about by creditors.

In the middle of a recession, tossed about by stimulus packages and bailouts.

The disciples fought the storm for nine cold, skin-drenching hours. And about 4:00 a.m. the unspeakable happened. They spotted someone coming on the water. " 'A ghost!' they said, crying out in terror" (v. 26 MSG).

They didn't expect Jesus to come to them this way.

Neither do we. We expect him to come in the form of peaceful hymns or Easter Sundays or quiet retreats. We expect to find Jesus in morning devotionals, church suppers, and meditation. We never expect to see him in a bear market, pink slip, lawsuit, foreclosure, or war. We never expect to see him in a storm. But it is in storms that he does his finest work, for it is in storms that he has our keenest attention.

Jesus replied to the disciples' fear with an invitation worthy of inscription on every church cornerstone and residential archway.

" 'Don't be afraid,' he said. 'Take courage. I am here!' " (v. 27 NLT).

Power inhabits those words. To awaken in an ICU and hear your husband say, "I am here." To lose your retirement yet feel the support of your family in the words "We are here." When a Little Leaguer spots Mom and Dad in the bleachers watching the game, "I am here" changes everything. Perhaps that's why God repeats the "I am here" pledge so often.

The Lord is near. (Phil. 4:5 NIV)

You are in me, and I am in you. (John 14:20 NIV)

I am with you always, to the very end of the age. (Matt. 28:20 NIV)

I give them eternal life, and they shall never perish; no one can snatch them out of my hand. (John 10:28 NIV)

Nothing can ever separate us from God's love. Neither death nor life, neither angels nor demons, neither our fears for today nor our worries about tomorrow — not even the powers of hell can separate us from God's love. (Rom. 8:38 NLT)

We cannot go where God is not. Look over your shoulder; that's God following you. Look into the storm; that's Christ coming toward you.

Much to Peter's credit, he took Jesus at his word. " 'Lord, if it is You, command me to come to You on the water.' So He said, 'Come.' And when Peter had come down out of the boat, he walked on the water to go to Jesus" (Matt. 14:28–29).

Peter never would have made this request on a calm sea. Had Christ strolled across a lake that was as smooth as mica, Peter would have applauded, but I doubt he would have stepped out of the boat. Storms prompt us to take unprecedented journeys. For a few historic steps and heart-stilling moments, Peter did the impossible. He defied every law of gravity and nature; "he walked on the water to go to Jesus."

My editors wouldn't have tolerated such brevity. They would have flooded the margin with red ink: "Elaborate! How quickly did Peter exit the boat? What were the other disciples doing? What was the expression on his face? Did he step on any fish?"

Matthew had no time for such questions. He moves us quickly to the major message of the event: where to stare in a storm. "But when [Peter] saw that the wind was boisterous, he was afraid; and beginning to sink he cried out, saying, 'Lord, save me!' " (v. 30).

A wall of water eclipsed his view. A wind gust snapped the mast with a crack and a slap. A flash of lightning illuminated the lake and the watery Appalachians it had become. Peter shifted his attention away from Jesus and toward the squall, and when he did, he sank like a brick in a pond. Give the storm waters more attention than the Storm Walker, and get ready to do the same.

Whether or not storms come, we cannot choose. But where we stare during a storm, that we can. I found a direct example of this truth while sitting in my cardiologist's office. My heart rate was misbehaving, taking the pace of a NASCAR race and the rhythm of a Morse code message. So I went to a specialist. After reviewing my tests and asking me some questions, the doctor nodded knowingly and told me to wait for him in his office.

I didn't like being sent to the principal's office as a kid. I don't like being sent to the doctor's office as a patient. But I went in, took a seat, and quickly noticed the doctor's abundant harvest of diplomas. They were everywhere, from everywhere. One degree from the university. Another degree from a residency. The third degree from his wife.

(I'm pausing to see if you caught the joke . . .)

The more I looked at his accomplishments, the better I felt. *I'm in good hands.* About the time I leaned back in the chair to relax, his nurse entered and handed me a sheet of paper. "The doctor will be in shortly," she explained. "In the meantime he wants you to acquaint yourself with this information. It summarizes your heart condition."

I lowered my gaze from the diplomas to the summary of the disorder. As I read, contrary winds began to blow. Unwelcome words like *atrial fibrillation, arrhythmia, embolic stroke,* and *blood clot* caused me to sink into my own Sea of Galilee.

What happened to my peace? I was feeling much better a moment ago. So I changed strategies. I counteracted diagnosis with diplomas. In between paragraphs of bad news, I looked at the wall for reminders of good news. That's what God wants us to do.

His call to courage is not a call to naïveté or ignorance. We aren't to be oblivious to the overwhelming challenges that life brings. We're to counterbalance them with long looks at God's accomplishments. "We must *pay much closer attention* to what we have heard, so that we do not drift away from it" (Heb. 2:1 NASB). Do whatever it takes to keep your gaze on Jesus.

When a friend of mine spent several days in the hospital at the bedside of her husband, she relied on hymns to keep her spirits up. Every few minutes she stepped into the restroom and sang a few verses of "Great Is Thy Faithfulness." Do likewise! Memorize scripture. Read biographies of great lives. Ponder the testimonies of faithful Christians. Make the deliberate decision to set your hope on him. Courage is always a possibility.

C. S. Lewis wrote a great paragraph on this thought:

> Faith . . . is the art of holding on to things your reason has once accepted, in spite of your changing moods. For moods will change, whatever view your reason takes. I know that by experience. Now that I am a Christian I do have moods in which the whole thing looks very improbable: but when I was an atheist I had moods in which Christianity looked terribly probable. . . . That is why Faith is such a necessary virtue: unless you teach your moods "where they get off," you can never be either a sound Christian or even a

sound atheist, but just a creature dithering to and fro, with its beliefs really dependent on the weather and the state of its digestion.[2]

Feed your fears, and your faith will starve. Feed your faith, and your fears will.

Jeremiah did this. Talk about a person caught in a storm! Slide down the timeline to the left about six hundred years, and learn a lesson from this Old Testament prophet. "I am the man who has seen affliction under the rod of [God's] wrath; he has driven and brought me into darkness without any light; surely against me he turns his hand again and again the whole day long" (Lam. 3:1–3 RSV).

Jeremiah was depressed, as gloomy as a giraffe with a neck ache. Jerusalem was under siege, his nation under duress. His world collapsed like a sand castle in a typhoon. He faulted God for his horrible emotional distress. He also blamed God for his physical ailments. "He [God] has made my flesh and my skin waste away, and broken my bones" (v. 4 RSV).

His body ached. His heart was sick. His faith was puny. "[God] has besieged and enveloped me with bitterness and tribulation" (v. 5 RSV). Jeremiah felt trapped like a man on a dead-end street. "He has walled me about so that I cannot escape; he has put heavy chains on me; though I call and cry for help, he shuts out my prayer; he has blocked my ways with hewn stones, he has made my paths crooked" (vv. 7–9 RSV).

Jeremiah could tell you the height of the waves and the speed of the wind. But then he realized how fast he was sinking. So he shifted his gaze. "But this I call to mind, and therefore I have hope: The steadfast love of the LORD never ceases, his mercies never come to an end; they are new every morning; great is thy faithfulness. 'The LORD is my portion,' says my soul, 'therefore I will hope in him' " (vv. 21–24 RSV).

"But this I call to mind . . ." Depressed, Jeremiah altered his thoughts, shifted his attention. He turned his eyes away from the waves and looked into the wonder of God. He quickly recited a quintet of promises. (I can envision him tapping these out on the five fingers of his hand.)

1. The steadfast love of the Lord never ceases.
2. His mercies never come to an end.
3. They are new every morning.
4. Great is thy faithfulness.
5. The Lord is my portion.

The storm didn't cease, but his discouragement did. So did Peter's. After a few moments of flailing in the water, he turned back to Christ and cried, " 'Lord, save me!' Immediately Jesus reached out his hand and caught him. 'You of little faith,' he said, 'why did you doubt?' And when they climbed into the boat, the wind died down" (Matt. 14:30–32 NIV).

Jesus could have stilled this storm hours earlier. But he didn't. He wanted to teach the followers a lesson. Jesus could have calmed your storm long ago too. But he hasn't. Does he also want to teach you a lesson? Could that lesson read something like this: "Storms are not an option, but fear is"?

God has hung his diplomas in the universe. Rainbows, sunsets, horizons, and star-sequincd skies. He has recorded his accomplishments in Scripture. We're not talking six thousand hours of flight time. His résumé includes Red Sea openings. Lions' mouths closings. Goliath topplings. Lazarus raisings. Storm stillings and strollings.

His lesson is clear. He's the commander of every storm. Are you scared in yours? Then stare at him. This may be your first flight. But it's certainly not his.

Your pilot has a call sign too: I Am Here.

■ ■ ■ ■

CHAPTER 7
THERE'S A DRAGON
IN MY CLOSET

■ ■ ■ ■

[Jesus] plunged into a sinkhole of
dreadful agony.
— MARK 14:33 MSG

FEAR OF WORST-CASE SCENARIOS

Next time an octopus traps you on the ocean floor, don't despair. Just launch into a flurry of somersaults. Unless you're wrapped in the grip of a fearfully strong arm or two, you'll escape with only a few sucker lesions.

As you ascend to the surface, you might encounter a shark. Don't panic; punch! Pound away at the eyes and gills. They are the most sensitive parts of its body.

The same holds true for alien encounters. Foil your next UFO abduction by going straight for the invader's eyes. Guard your thoughts, however, as space creatures may be able to read your mind.

Though gorillas can't read your mind, they can lock you in their grasp. The grip of a silverback is padlock tight. Your only hope of escape is to stroke its arm while loudly smacking your lips. Primates are fastidious groomers. Hopefully, the gorilla will interpret your actions as a spa treatment.

If not, things could be worse. You could be falling from the sky in a malfunctioning parachute, trapped in a plummeting elevator, or buried alive in a steel coffin. You could be facing your worst-case scenario. We all have them: situations of ultimate desperation. That's why *The Complete Worst-Case Scenario Survival Handbook*[1] has been such a success.

Thanks to the book, I now know how to react to a grabbing gorilla or an abducting alien. The odds of such occasions are so remote, however, I've lost no sleep over them. I have stayed awake pondering other gloomy possibilities.

Growing senile is one. The thought of growing old doesn't trouble me. Don't mind losing my youth, hair, or teeth. But the thought of losing my mind? Dreadful. To visit an Alzheimer's unit is a disturbing thing. Silver-haired elderly staring blankly into space, asking dementia-driven questions. I don't want to end up that way.

Failing to provide for my family has haunted me. In another worst-case scenario my wife, Denalyn, outlives me and our savings and is destitute, dependent upon the generosity of some kind stranger. She tells me to dismiss such thoughts, that my concerns are folly. Easier said than done, I reply.

These lurking fears. These uninvited Loch Ness monsters. Not pedestrian anxieties of daily deadlines and common colds, but the lingering horror of some inescapable talon. Illogical and inexplicable, perhaps, but also undeniable.

What's your worst fear? A fear of public failure, unemployment, or heights? The fear that you'll never find the right spouse or enjoy good health? The fear of being trapped, abandoned, or forgotten?

These are real fears, born out of legitimate concerns. Yet left unchecked, they metastasize into obsessions. The step between prudence and paranoia is short and steep. Prudence wears a seat belt. Paranoia avoids cars. Prudence washes with soap. Paranoia avoids human contact. Prudence saves for old age. Paranoia hoards even trash. Prudence prepares and plans. Paranoia panics. Prudence calculates the risk and takes the plunge. Paranoia never enters the water.

The words *plunge* and *water* come to mind as I'm writing this chapter while sitting on the edge of a hotel swimming pool. (Amazing what a hot sun, a cool soda, and a pool chair can do for creativity.) A father and his two small daughters are at play. He's in the water; they jump into his arms. Let me restate that: one jumps; the other ponders. The dry one gleefully watches her sister leap. She dances up and down as the other splashes. But when her dad invites her to do the same, she shakes her head and backs away.

A living parable! How many people spend life on the edge of the pool? Consulting caution. Ignoring faith. Never taking the plunge. Happy to experience life vicariously through others. Preferring to take no risk rather than any risk. For fear of the worst, they never enjoy life at its best.

By contrast, their sister jumps. Not with foolish abandon, but with belief in the goodness of a father's heart and trust in a father's arms. Such was the choice of Jesus. He did more than speak about fear. He faced it.

The decisive acts of the gospel drama are played out on two stages — Gethsemane's garden and Golgotha's cross. Friday's cross witnessed the severest suffering. Thursday's garden staged the profoundest fear. It was here, amidst the olive trees, that Jesus "fell to the ground. He prayed that, if it were possible, the awful hour awaiting him might pass him by. 'Abba, Father,' he cried out, 'everything is possible for you. Please take this cup of suffering away from me. Yet I want your will to be done, not mine' "

(Mark 14:35–36 NLT).

A reader once called me both on the phone and on the carpet because of what I wrote on this passage. He didn't appreciate the way I described Christ as having "eyes wide with a stupor of fear."[2] I told him he needed to take his complaint to a higher level. Gospel-writer Mark is the one who paints the picture of Jesus as pale faced and trembling. "Horror . . . came over him" (Mark 14:33 NEB). The word *horror* is "used of a man who is rendered helpless, disoriented, who is agitated and anguished by the threat of some approaching event."[3]

Matthew agreed. He described Jesus as

depressed and confused (Matt. 26:37[4]);

sorrowful and troubled (RSV);

anguish[ed] and dismay[ed] (NEB).

We've never seen Christ like this. Not in the Galilean storm, at the demoniac's necropolis, or on the edge of the Nazarene cliff. We've never heard such screams from his voice or seen his eyes this wide. And never, ever, have we read a sentence like this: "He plunged into a sinkhole of dreadful agony" (Mark 14:33 MSG). This is a

121

weighty moment. God has become flesh, and Flesh is feeling fear full bore. Why? Of what was Jesus afraid?

It had something to do with a cup. "Please take this cup of suffering away from me." *Cup,* in biblical terminology, was more than a drinking utensil. *Cup* equaled God's anger, judgment, and punishment. When God took pity on apostate Jerusalem, he said, "See, I have taken out of your hand the cup that made you stagger . . . the goblet of my wrath" (Isa. 51:22 NIV). Through Jeremiah, God declared that all nations would drink of the cup of his disgust: "Take from my hand this cup filled to the brim with my anger, and make all the nations to whom I send you drink from it" (Jer. 25:15 NLT). According to John, those who dismiss God "must drink the wine of God's anger. It has been poured full strength into God's cup of wrath. And they will be tormented with fire and burning sulfur in the presence of the holy angels and the Lamb" (Rev. 14:10 NLT).

The cup equaled Jesus' worst-case scenario: to be the recipient of God's wrath. He had never felt God's fury, didn't deserve to. He'd never experienced isolation from his Father; the two had been one for eternity. He'd never known physical death; he was an immortal being. Yet within a few short hours, Jesus would face them all. God would unleash his sin-hating wrath on the sin-covered Son. And Jesus was afraid. Deathly afraid. And what he did with his fear shows us what to do with ours.

He prayed. He told his followers, "Sit here while I go and pray over there" (Matt. 26:36). One prayer was inadequate. "Again, a second time, He went away and prayed . . . and prayed the third time, saying the same words" (vv. 42, 44). He even requested the prayer support of his friends. "Stay awake and pray for strength," he urged (v. 41 NCV).

Jesus faced his ultimate fear with honest prayer.

Let's not overcomplicate this topic. Don't we do so? We prescribe words for prayer, places for prayer, clothing for prayer, postures for prayer; durations, intonations, and incantations. Yet Jesus' garden appeal had none of these. It was brief (twenty-six English words), straightforward ("Please take this cup of suffering away"), and trusting ("Yet I want your will to be done, not mine"). Low on slick and high on authentic. Less a silver-tongued saint in the sanctuary; more a frightened child in a father's lap.

That's it. Jesus' garden prayer is a child's prayer. *Abba,* he prayed, using the homespun word a child would use while scampering up on the lap of Papa.

My father let me climb onto his lap . . . when he drove! He'd be arrested for doing so today. But half a century ago no one cared. Especially in a flat-as-a-skillet West Texas oil field, where rabbits outnumber people. Who cares if little Max sits on Dad's lap as he drives the company truck (oops, sorry, Exxon) from rig to rig?

I loved it. Did it matter that I couldn't see over the dash? That my feet stopped two feet shy of the brake and accelerator? That I didn't know a radio from a carburetor? By no means. I helped my dad drive his truck.

There were occasions when he even let me select the itinerary. At an intersection he would offer, "Right or left, Max?" I'd lift my freckled face and peer over the steering wheel, consider my options, and make my choice.

And do so with gusto, whipping the wheel like a race car driver at Monte Carlo. Did I fear driving into the ditch? Overturning the curve? Running the tire into a rut? By no means. Dad's hands were next to mine, his eyes keener than mine. Consequently, I was fearless! Anyone can drive a car from the lap of a father.

And anyone can pray from the same perspective.

Prayer is the practice of sitting calmly in God's lap and placing our hands on his steering wheel. He handles the speed and hard curves and ensures safe arrival. And we offer our requests; we ask God to "take this cup away." This cup of disease, betrayal, financial collapse, joblessness, conflict, or senility. Prayer is this simple. And such simple prayer equipped Christ to stare down his deepest fear.

Do likewise. Fight your dragons in Gethsemane's garden. Those persistent, ugly villains of the heart — talk to God about them.

I don't want to lose my spouse, Lord. Help me to fear less and trust you more.

I have to fly tomorrow, Lord, and I can't sleep for fear some terrorist will get on board and take down the plane. Won't you remove this fear?

The bank just called and is about to foreclose on our home. What's going to happen to my family? Can you teach me to trust?

I'm scared, Lord. The doctor just called, and the news is not good. You know what's ahead for me. I give my fear to you.

Be specific about your fears. Identify what "this cup" is and talk to God about it. Putting your worries into words disrobes them. They look silly standing there naked.

Yann Martel points this out in his novel *Life of Pi.* The main character, Pi, finds himself adrift at sea on a twenty-six-foot lifeboat with a 450-pound Bengal tiger as a companion. Pi ended up in this plight when his father, a zookeeper, went broke and loaded the family on a Japanese ship headed to Canada. The ship sank, leaving Pi and the tiger (named Richard Parker) alone on the ocean. While on the lifeboat, Pi begins to analyze his fears, both of the sea and the tiger.

I must say a word about fear. It is life's only true opponent. Only fear can defeat life. It is a clever, treacherous adversary, how well I know. It has no decency, respects no law or convention, shows no mercy. It goes for your weakest spot, which it finds with unerring ease. It begins in your mind, always. One moment you are feeling calm, self-possessed, happy. Then fear, disguised in the garb of mild-mannered doubt, slips into your mind like a spy. Doubt meets disbelief and disbelief tries to push it out. But disbelief is a poorly armed foot soldier. Doubt does away with it with little trouble. You become anxious. Reason comes to do battle for you. You are reassured. Reason is fully equipped with the latest weapons technology. But, to your amazement, despite superior tactics and a number of undeniable victories, reason is laid low. You feel yourself weakening, wavering. Your anxiety becomes dread. . . .

Quickly you make rash decisions. You dismiss your last allies: hope and trust. There, you've defeated yourself. Fear, which is but an impression, has triumphed over you.[5]

Pi realizes that fear cannot be reasoned with. Logic doesn't talk fear off the ledge or onto the airplane. So what does? How can one avoid that towel-in-the-ring surrender to the enemy? Pi gives this counsel:

You must fight hard to express it. You must fight hard to shine the light of words upon it. Because if you don't, if your fear becomes a wordless darkness that you avoid, perhaps even manage to forget, you open yourself to further attacks of fear because you never truly fought the opponent who defeated you.[6]

It's our duty to pull back the curtains, to expose our fears, each and every one. Like vampires, they can't stand the sunlight. Financial fears, relationship fears, professional fears, safety fears — call them out in prayer. Drag them out by the hand of your mind, and make them stand before God and take their comeuppance!

Jesus made his fears public. He "offered up prayers and petitions with loud cries and tears to the one who could save him from death" (Heb. 5:7 NIV). He prayed loudly enough to be heard and recorded, and he begged his community of friends to pray with him.

His prayer in the garden becomes, for Christians, a picture of the church in action — a place where fears can be verbalized, pronounced, stripped down, and denounced; an escape from the "wordless darkness" of suppressed frights. A healthy church is where our fears go to die. We pierce them through with Scripture, psalms of celebration and lament. We melt them in the sunlight of confession. We extinguish them with the waterfall of worship, choosing to gaze at God, not our dreads.

The next time you find yourself facing a worst-case moment, do this. Verbalize your angst to a trusted circle of God-seekers. This is an essential step. Find your version of Peter, James, and John. (One hopes yours will stay awake longer.) The big deal (and good news) is this: you needn't live alone with your fear.

Besides, what if your fears are nothing more than the devil's hoax? A hell-hatched, joy-stealing prank?

I have a friend who was dreading a letter from the IRS. According to their early calculation, he owed them money, money he did not have. He was told to expect a letter detailing the amount. When the letter arrived, his courage failed him. He couldn't bear to open it, so the envelope sat on his desk for five days while he writhed in dread. How much could it be? Where would he get the funds? For how long would he be sent to prison? Finally he summoned the gumption to open the envelope. He found, not a bill to be paid, but a check to be cashed. The IRS, as it turned out, owed him money! He had wasted five days on needless fear. There are very few monsters who warrant the fear we have of them.

As followers of God, you and I have a huge asset. We know everything is going to turn out all right. Christ hasn't budged from his throne, and Romans 8:28 hasn't evaporated from the Bible. Our problems have always been his possibilities. The kidnapping of Joseph resulted in the preservation of his family. The persecution of Daniel led to a cabinet position. Christ entered the world by a surprise pregnancy and redeemed it through his unjust murder. Dare we believe what the Bible teaches? That no disaster is ultimately fatal?

Chrysostom did. He was the archbishop of Constantinople from AD 398 to 404. He gained a following by his eloquent criticisms of the wealthy and powerful. Twice banished by the authorities, he once asked: "What can I fear? Will it be death? But you know that Christ is my life, and that I shall gain by death. Will it be exile? But the earth and all its fulness is the Lord's. Will it be the loss of wealth? But we have brought nothing into the world, and can carry nothing out. Thus all the terrors of the world are contemptible in my eyes; and I smile at all its good things. Poverty I do not fear; riches I do not sigh for. Death I do not shrink from."[7]

The apostle Paul would have applauded that paragraph. He penned his final words in the bowels of a Roman prison, chained to a guard — within earshot of his executioner's footsteps. Worst-case scenario? Not from Paul's perspective. "God's looking after me, keeping me safe in the kingdom of heaven. All praise to him, praise forever!" (2 Tim. 4:18 MSG).

Paul chose to trust his Father.

By the way, I'm happy to report that the poolside girl has chosen to believe hers. After extensive coaxing from her dad and coaching from her sister, she held her nose and jumped. Last tally, she's taken at least a dozen plunges. Good for her. Another fear has fallen victim to trust.

■ ■ ■ ■

CHAPTER 8
THIS BRUTAL
PLANET

■ ■ ■ ■

Do not fear those who kill the body but cannot kill the soul.

— MATTHEW 10:28

FEAR OF VIOLENCE

The greatest golfer in the history of the sport sat down to eat his breakfast, never suspecting it would be his last. Byron Nelson had slept well the night before, better than he had in days. He had showered, shaved, and then smiled when his wife, Peggy, announced the meal of the morning: sausage, biscuits, and eggs.

He was ninety-four years old, sixty-one years removed from the streak: eleven consecutive tournament victories. Tiger Woods has won six in a row. Arnold Palmer won three; so did Sam Snead, Ben Hogan, and a few others. But Nelson's record of eleven straight stands out like an oak tree in a wheat field. He retired a year later and bought a ranch near Fort Worth, Texas, where he lived peacefully until God called him home September 26, 2006.

After washing the dishes, he sat down to listen to a favorite Christian radio broadcast.

Peggy left for Bible study at the church. ("I'm so proud of you," he told her.) She returned a few hours later to find him on the floor. No sign of pain or struggle. His good heart had just stopped.[1]

Russia of the early 1950s needed little excuse to imprison her citizens. Let a person question a decision of Stalin or speak against the Communist regime, and he could find himself walking the frozen tundra behind the barbed wires of a Soviet concentration camp. Boris Kornfeld did. No known record of his crime survives, only the sketchy details of his life. Born a Jew. Trained as a physician and befriended by a believer in Christ.

With ample time on their hands, the two men engaged in long, rigorous discussions. Kornfeld began to connect the promised Messiah of the old covenant with the Nazarene of the new. Following Jesus went against every fiber of his ancestry, but in the end he chose to do so.

The decision cost him his life.

He saw a guard stealing bread from a dying man. Prior to his conversion, Kornfeld never would have reported the crime. Now his conscience compelled him to do so. It was only a matter of time before the other guards would get even. Kornfeld, even in danger, was at complete peace. For the first time in his life, he had no fear of death or eternity. His only desire was to tell someone about his discovery before he lost his life.

An opportunity came in the form of a cancer patient, a fellow prisoner who was recovering from abdominal surgery. Left alone with him in the recovery room, Kornfeld urgently whispered his story. He poured out every detail. The young man was stirred yet so groggy from the anesthesia that he fell asleep. When he awoke, he asked to see the physician. It was too late. During the night someone had dealt the doctor eight blows on the head with a plasterer's hammer. Colleagues had tried to save his life but couldn't.[2]

Byron Nelson and Boris Kornfeld embraced the same convictions. They anchored their hope to the same rock and set their sights on the same heaven and trusted the same Savior. Yet one passed into heaven on a pathway of peace, the other through a maelstrom of brutality.

Given the choice, I'd go out like Mr. Nelson.

The unnamed heroes of Hebrews would have as well. Their stories occupy a curious paragraph toward the end of the patriarch parade. They follow the better-known names of Abel, who though "being dead still speaks" (Heb. 11:4); Enoch, who "did not see death" (v. 5); Noah, who "became heir of the righteousness" (v. 7); Abraham and Sarah, whose descendants are as "innumerable as the sand which is by the seashore" (v. 12).

A person might read this far and draw a conclusion. God rewards faithful lives with serenity and storied legacies. Live well. Live and die peacefully. Right? Then verses 35–37 present the hard side: "Others were tortured, not accepting deliverance, that they might obtain a better resurrection. Still others had trials of mockings and scourgings, yes, and of chains and imprisonment. They were stoned, they were sawn in two, were tempted, were slain with the sword. They wandered about in sheepskins and goatskins, being destitute, afflicted, tormented."

Contrary to what we'd hope, good people aren't exempt from violence. Murderers don't give the godly a pass. Rapists don't vet victims according to spiritual résumés. The bloodthirsty and wicked don't skip over the heavenbound. We aren't insulated. But neither are we intimidated. Jesus has a word or two about this brutal world: "Do not fear those who kill the body but cannot kill the soul" (Matt. 10:28).

The disciples needed this affirmation. Jesus had just told them to expect scourging, trials, death, hatred, and persecution (vv. 17–23). Not the kind of locker room pep talk that rallies the team. To their credit none defected. Perhaps they didn't because of the fresh memory of Jesus' flexed muscles in the graveyard. Jesus had taken his disciples to "the other side into the country of the Gadarenes, [where] two men who were demon-possessed met Him as they were coming out of the tombs. They were so extremely violent that no one could pass by that way. And they cried out, saying, 'What business do we have with each other, Son of God? Have You come here to torment us before the time?' " (Matt. 8:28–29 NASB).

The most dramatic and immediate reactions to the presence of God on earth emerged from demons like these — the numberless, invisible, sexless, fiendish djinns of Satan. These two men were demon possessed and, consequently, "extremely violent." People walked wide detours around the cemetery to avoid them.

Not Jesus. He marched in as if he owned the place. The stunned demons never expected to see Jesus here in the devil's digs on the foreign side of Galilee, the region of pagans and pigs. Jews avoided such haunts. Jesus didn't.

The demons and Jesus needed no introduction. They had battled it out somewhere else, and the demons had no interest in a rematch. They didn't even put up a fight. "Have you come to punish us before our time?" (v. 29 CEV). Backpedaling. Stuttering. Translation? "We know you will put it to us in the end, but do we get double trouble in the meantime?" They crumpled like stringless puppets. Pathetic, their appeal: "Please send us into those pigs!" (v. 31 CEV).

Jesus did so. "Move," he exorcised. No shout, scream, incantation, dance, incense, or demand. Just one small word. He who sustains the worlds with a word directs demonic traffic with the same.

And though this world, with devils filled,
should threaten to undo us,
we will not fear, for God hath willed
His truth to triumph through us.
The Prince of Darkness grim,
we tremble not for him;
his rage we can endure,
for lo, his doom is sure;

one little word shall fell him.[3]

The contest between good and evil lasted a matter of seconds. Christ is fire, and demons are rats on the ship. They scurried overboard at first heat.

This is the balance on which Jesus writes the check of courage: "Do not fear those who kill the body but cannot kill the soul" (Matt. 10:28). You indwell the garrison of God's guardianship. "Can anything separate us from the love Christ has for us? Can troubles or problems or sufferings or hunger or nakedness or danger or violent death? . . . Nothing above us, nothing below us, nor anything else in the whole world will ever be able to separate us from the love of God that is in Christ Jesus our Lord" (Rom. 8:35, 39 NCV).

Courage emerges, not from increased police security, but from enhanced spiritual maturity. Martin Luther King exemplified this. He chose not to fear those who meant him harm. On April 3, 1968, he spent hours in a plane, waiting on the tarmac, due to bomb threats. When he arrived in Memphis later that day, he was tired and hungry but not afraid.

"We've got some difficult days ahead," he told the crowd. "But it doesn't matter with me now. Because I've been to the mountaintop. And I don't mind. Like anybody, I would like to live a long life. Longevity has its place. But I'm not concerned about that now. I just want to do God's will. And He's allowed me to go up to the mountain. And I've looked over. And I've seen the promised land. I may not get there with you. But I want you to know tonight that we, as a people, will get to the promised land. And I'm happy tonight. I'm not worried about anything. I'm not fearing any man. Mine eyes have seen the glory of the coming of the Lord."[4]

He would be dead in less than twenty-four hours. But the people who meant him harm fell short in their goal. They took his breath, but they never took his soul.

In his award-winning book on the Rwandan genocide of 1994, Philip Gourevitch tells the story of Thomas, a Tutsi marked for slaughter. He was one of the few who escaped the machete-wielding Hutu murderers.

Thomas told me that he had been trained as a Boy Scout "to look at danger, and study it, but not to be afraid," and I was struck that each of his encounters with Hutu Power had followed a pattern: when the minister ordered him back to work, when the soldiers came for him, and when they told him to sit on the street, Thomas always refused before complying. The killers were accustomed to encountering fear, and Thomas had always acted as if there must be some misunderstanding for anyone to feel the need to threaten him.[5]

Evildoers have less chance of hurting you if you aren't already a victim. "Fearing people is a dangerous trap, but trusting the LORD means safety" (Prov. 29:25 NLT). Remember, "his angels . . . guard you" (Ps. 91:11 NIV). He is your "refuge" (Ps. 62:8), your "hiding place" (Ps. 32:7), your "fortress" (2 Sam. 22:2–3). "The LORD is on my side; I will not fear. What can man do to me?" (Ps. 118:6). Satan cannot reach you without passing through him.

Then what are we to make of the occasions Satan does reach us? How are we supposed to understand the violence listed in Hebrews 11 or the tragic end of Boris Kornfeld? Or, most supremely, how are we to understand the suffering of Jesus? Ropes. Whips. Thorns. Nails. These trademarked his final moments. Do you hear the whip slapping against his back, ripping sinew from bone? Thirty-nine times the leather slices, first the air, then the skin. Jesus clutches the post and groans, battered by wave after wave of violence. Soldiers force a thorny wreath over his brow, sting his face with slaps, coat it with saliva. They load a beam on his shoulders and force him to march up a hill. This is the condemned sharpening his own guillotine, tying his own noose, wiring his own electric chair. Jesus shouldered his own tool of execution. The cross.

Cicero referred to crucifixion as "a most cruel and disgusting punishment."[6] In polite Roman society the word *cross* was an obscenity, not to be uttered in conversation. Roman soldiers were exempt from crucifixion except in matters of treason. It was ugly and vile, harsh and degrading. And it was the manner by which Jesus chose to die. "He humbled himself and became obedient to death — even death on a cross!" (Phil. 2:8 NIV).

A calmer death would have sufficed. A single drop of blood could have redeemed humankind. Shed his blood, silence his breath, still his pulse, but be quick about it. Plunge a sword into his heart. Take a dagger to his neck. Did the atonement for sin demand six hours of violence?

No, but his triumph over sadism did. Jesus

once and for all displayed his authority over savagery. Evil may have her moments, but they will be brief. Satan unleashed his meanest demons on God's Son. He tortured every nerve ending and inflicted every misery. Yet the master of death could not destroy the Lord of life. Heaven's best took hell's worst and turned it into hope.

I pray God spares you such evil. May he grant you the long life and peaceful passage of a Byron Nelson. But if he doesn't, if you "have been given not only the privilege of trusting in Christ but also the privilege of suffering for him" (Phil. 1:29 NLT), remember, God wastes no pain.

Consider Boris Kornfeld, the Russian physician bludgeoned to death because of his convictions. Though the doctor died, his testimony survived. The man with whom he spoke never forgot the conversation.

There, in the quiet camp hospital recovery room, the doctor sat by his patient's bedside, dispensing compassion and peace. Dr. Kornfeld passionately related the story of his conversion to Chritianity, his words flavored with conviction. The patient was hot and feverish, yet alert enough to ponder Dr. Kornfeld's words. He would later write that he sensed a "mystical knowledge" in the doctor's voice.

The "mystical knowledge" transformed the young patient. He embraced Kornfeld's Christ and later celebrated in verse with this joyous affirmation:

God of Universe! I believe again![7]

The patient survived the camps and began to write about his prison experience, disclosing the gulag horror. One exposé after another: *One Day in the Life of Ivan Denisovich, The Gulag Archipelago, Live Not by Lies.* Some attribute the collapse of Eastern Communism, in part, to his writings. But were it not for the suffering of Kornfeld, we'd have never known the brilliance of his young convert: Alexander Solzhenitsyn.

What man meant for evil, God, yet again, used for good.

■ ■ ■ ■

CHAPTER 9
MAKE-BELIEVE
MONEY

■ ■ ■ ■

Do not fear, little flock, for it is your Father's good pleasure to give you the kingdom.

— LUKE 12:32

FEAR OF THE COMING WINTER

A Monopoly champion sits in your office. The Michael Phelps of the game board. The Pelé of the Boardwalk. He spends all day every day slam-dunking the competition, collecting houses, Park Places, and make-believe money the way Solomon collected wives. He never goes to jail, always passes Go, and has permanent addresses on Illinois and Kentucky avenues. If the Fortune 500 ranked Monopoly billionaires, this guy would out-Buffett Warren Buffett. No one has more money than he.

And he wants you to help him invest it. You are, after all, a financial planner. You speak the language of stocks and annuities, have ample experience with IRAs, mutual funds, and securities. But all your experience didn't prepare you for this request. Yet here he sits in your office, encircled by bags of pink cash and little plastic buildings. Invest Monopoly earnings?

149

"I have 314 Park Places, 244 Boardwalks, and enough Reading Railroads to circle the globe like thread on a spool."

Is this guy for real? You do your best to be polite. "Seems you've amassed quite a Monopoly fortune."

He crosses his arms and smiles. "Indeed I have. And I'm ready for you to put it to work. It's time for me to sit back and take it easy. Let someone else monopolize Monopoly for a while."

You take another look at his stacks of funny money and toy real estate and abandon all tact. "Sir, you're crazy. Your currency has no value. Your cash has no clout. Outside of your game, it's worthless. I'm sorry to tell you this, but you've made a foolish mistake. In fact, you are a fool."

Strong language. But if you choose to use it, you are in the company of God.

And [Jesus] told them this parable: "The ground of a certain rich man produced a good crop. He thought to himself, 'What shall I do? I have no place to store my crops.'

"Then he said, 'This is what I'll do. I will tear down my barns and build bigger ones, and there I will store all my grain and my goods. And I'll say to myself, "You have plenty of good things laid up for many years. Take life easy; eat, drink and be merry.'

"But God said to him, 'You fool! This very night your life will be demanded from you. Then who will get what you have prepared for yourself?'

"This is how it will be with anyone who stores up things for himself but is not rich toward God." (Luke 12:16–21 NIV)

He seemed to be a decent fellow, this wealthy farmer. Sharp enough to turn a profit, savvy enough to enjoy a windfall. For all we know he made his fortune honestly. No mention is made of exploitation or embezzlement. He put his God-given talent to making talents and succeeded. Flush with success, he resolved to learn a lesson from the fable of the ant and the grasshopper.

The grasshopper, you'll remember, wondered why the ant worked so hard in the summer day. "Why not come and chat with me instead of toiling in that way?" The ant explained his labor: "I'm helping to lay up food for the winter and recommend you do the same." But the grasshopper preferred to flitter than work. So while the ant prepared, the grasshopper played. And when winter brought its harsh winds and barren fields, the ant nibbled on corn while the grasshopper stood on the street corner holding a cardboard sign: "Any work will do. I'll hop right to it."

The tycoon in Jesus' story wasn't about to play the role of the grasshopper. No food lines or soup kitchens for him. And no food lines or soup kitchens for us either. We empathize with the fecund farmer. Truth be told, we want to learn from his success. Has he written a book (*Bigger Barns for Retirement*)? Does he conduct seminars ("Recession- Proof Your Barn in Twelve Easy Steps")? Doesn't the barn stuffer model responsible planning? And yet Jesus crowns him with the pointy hat of the dunce. Where did the guy mess up? Jesus answers by populating three paragraphs with a swarm of personal pronouns. Reread the heart of the parable, noting the heart of the investor:

And *he* thought to *himself,* saying, "What shall *I* do since *I* have no room to store *my* crops?" So *he* said, "*I* will do this: *I* will pull down *my* barns and build greater ones, and there *I* will store all *my* crops and all *my* goods. And *I* will say to *my* soul, 'Soul, *you* have many goods laid up for many years; take *your* ease, eat, drink,

This rich man indwelled a one-room house of mirrors. He looked north, south, east, and west and saw the same individual — himself. I. I. My. I. I. My. I. My. My. I. My. No *they.* No *thee.* Just *me.* Even when he said *you,* he spoke to himself. "You have many goods. Take your ease."

And so he did. He successfully hoarded enough stuff so he could wine, dine, and recline. He moved to Scottsdale, bought a five-bedroom split-level on the third fairway of the country club. He unpacked the moving vans, set up his bank accounts, pulled on his swimming trunks, and dove into the backyard pool. Too bad he forgot to fill it with water. He popped his skull on the concrete and woke up in the presence of God, who was anything but impressed with his portfolio. "Fool! This night your soul will be required of you; then whose will those things be which you have provided?" (v. 20).

The rich fool went to the wrong person ("He thought to himself") and asked the wrong question ("What shall I do?"). His error was not that he planned but rather that his plans didn't include God. Jesus criticized not the man's affluence but his arrogance, not the presence of personal goals but the absence of God in those goals. What if he'd taken his money to the right person (God) with the right question ("What do you want me to do?")?

Accumulation of wealth is a popular defense against fear. Since we fear losing our jobs, health care, or retirement benefits, we amass possessions, thinking the more we have, the safer we are. The same insecurity motivated Babel's tower builders. The nations that spread out after Noah's flood decided to circle their wagons. "Come, let us build ourselves a city, and a tower whose top is in the heavens; let us make a name for ourselves, lest we be scattered abroad over the face of the whole earth" (Gen. 11:4).

Do you detect the fear in those words? The people feared being scattered and separated. Yet rather than turn to God, they turned to stuff. They accumulated and stacked. They collected and built. News of their efforts would reach the heavens and keep their enemies at a distance. The city motto of Babel was this: "The more you hoard, the safer you are." So they hoarded. They heaped stones and mortar and bricks and mutual funds and IRAs and savings accounts. They stockpiled pensions, possessions, and property. Their tower of stuff grew so tall they got neck aches looking at it.

"We are safe!" they announced at the ribbon-cutting ceremony.

"No you aren't," God corrected. And the Babel-builders began to babble. The city of one language became the glossolalia of the United Nations minus the interpreters. Doesn't God invoke identical correction today? We engineer stock and investment levies, take cover behind the hedge of hedge funds. We trust annuities and pensions to the point that balance statements determine our mood levels. But then come the Katrina-level recessions and downturns, and the confusion begins all over again.

During the economic collapse of October 2008, a Stamford, Connecticut, man threatened to blow up a bank. When he lost $500,000 of his $2,000,000 portfolio, he planned to bring a gun into the facility and take the lives of innocent people if necessary.[1] As if a shooting spree would do anything to restore his loss. Fear has never been famous for its logic.

If there were no God, stuff-trusting would be the only appropriate response to an uncertain future. But there is a God. And this God does not want his children to trust money. He responded to the folly of the rich man with a flurry of "Do not worry" appeals. "Do not worry about your life. . . . Do not seek what you should eat or what you should drink, nor have an anxious mind" (vv. 22, 29).

Don't follow the path of the wealthy bumpkin who was high on financial cents but impoverished of spiritual sense. Instead, "Do not fear, *little flock,* for it is your Father's good pleasure to give you the kingdom" (v. 32). This is the only occasion when Jesus calls us his "little flock." The discussion of provision prompts such pastoral concern.

I once rode on horseback with a shepherdess through the Black Mountains of Wales. The green valleys were cotton-puffed with heads of sheep. We came upon one member of the flock that had gotten herself into quite a fix. She was stuck on her back in the rut of a dirt road and couldn't stand up.

When the shepherdess saw her, she dismounted from her horse, looked at me, and chuckled. "They aren't the brightest of beasts." She righted the animal, and off it ran.

We aren't the brightest of beasts either. Yet we have a shepherd who will get us back on our feet. Like a good shepherd, he will not let us go unclothed or unfed. "I have never seen the godly abandoned or their children begging for bread" (Ps. 37:25 NLT). What a welcome reminder! When homes foreclose or pensions evaporate, we need a shepherd. In Christ we have one. And his "good pleasure [is] to *give* you the kingdom."

Giving characterizes God's creation. From the first page of Scripture, he is presented as a philanthropic creator. He produces in pluralities: stars, plants, birds, and animals. Every gift arrives in bulk, multiples, and medleys. God begets Adam and Eve into a "liturgy of abundance"[2] and tells them to follow suit: "be fruitful and multiply" (Gen. 1:28).

Scrooge didn't create the world; God did.

Psalm 104 celebrates this lavish creation with twenty-three verses of itemized blessings: the heavens and the earth, the waters and streams and trees and birds and goats and wine and oil and bread and people and lions. God is the source of "innumerable teeming things, living things both small and great. . . . These all wait for You, that You may give them their food in due season" (vv. 25, 27).

And he does. God is the great giver. The great provider. The fount of every blessing.

Absolutely generous and utterly dependable. The resounding and recurring message of Scripture is clear: God owns it all. God shares it all. Trust him, not stuff!

> Command those who are rich in this present age not to be haughty, nor to trust in uncertain riches but in the living God, who gives us richly all things to enjoy. Let them do good, that they be rich in good works, ready to give, willing to share, storing up for themselves a good foundation for the time to come, that they may lay hold on eternal life. (1 Tim. 6:17–19)

Are you "rich in this present age"? If you have the resources and education to read this book, you are. Almost half the world — more than three billion people — live on less than $2.50 a day.[3] If your income is higher, then you are rich, and your affluence demands double vigilance.

"Adversity is sometimes hard upon a man," wrote Thomas Carlyle, "but for one man who can stand prosperity, there are a hundred that will stand adversity."[4] The abundance of possessions has a way of eclipsing God, no matter how meager those possessions may be. There is a predictable progression from poverty to pride. The poor man prays and works; God hears and blesses. The humble man becomes rich and forgets God. The faithful, poor man becomes the proud, rich man. As God said through Hosea, "When I fed them, they were satisfied; when they were satisfied, they became proud; then they forgot me" (Hos. 13:6 NIV). The proud, rich man falls under God's judgment. How can we avoid this? How can a person survive prosperity?

Do not be haughty . . . Do not think for a moment that you had anything to do with your accumulation. Scripture makes one thing clear. Your stocks, cash, and 401(k)? They are not yours.

> To the LORD your God belong the heavens, even the highest heavens, the earth and everything in it. (Deut. 10:14 NIV)

> Yours, O LORD, is the greatness and the power and the glory and the majesty and the splendor, for everything in heaven and earth is yours. (1 Chron. 29:11 NIV)

> "The silver is mine and the gold is mine," declares the LORD Almighty. (Hag. 2:8 NIV)

The rich fool in Jesus' story missed this point. The wise woman Jesus spotted in the temple did not. "Then a poor widow came and dropped in two small coins. Jesus called his disciples to him and said, 'I tell you the truth, this poor widow has given more than all the others who are making contributions. For they gave a tiny part of their surplus, but she, poor as she is, has given everything she had to live on' " (Mark 12:42–44 NLT).

The dear woman was down to her last pennies, yet rather than spend them on bread, she returned them to God. Wall Street financial gurus would have urged her to cut back on her giving. In fact, the investment counselors would have applauded the investment strategy of the barn builder and discouraged the generosity of the lady. Jesus did just the opposite. His hero of financial stewardship was a poor woman who placed her entire portfolio in the offering plate.

Do not put your "trust in uncertain riches." Or, as one translation reads, "[the rich] must not be haughty nor set their hope on riches — that unstable foundation" (1 Tim. 6:17 WEY). Money is an untrustworthy foundation. The United States economy endured ten recessions between 1948 and 2001. These downturns lasted an average of ten months apiece and resulted in the loss of billions of dollars.[5] Every five years or so, the economy dumps its suitors and starts over. What would you think of a man who did the same with women? What word would you use to describe a husband who philandered his way through nine different wives over fifty years?

And what word would you use to describe wife number ten? How about this one? *Fool.* Those who trust money are foolish. They are setting themselves up to be duped and dumped into a dystopia of unhappiness. Have you ever noticed that the word *miser* is just one letter short of the word *misery?*

Bob Russell learned the connection between the two words. He relates this great story:

A few years ago our family got involved in a game of Monopoly. I was on a roll. First time around I stopped on Illinois Avenue and Park Place and bought them both. Then I added Indiana Avenue and Boardwalk. Let anyone come down that street and I had them dead. I bought all four railroads. I had houses and hotels; I couldn't keep from smirking. I had so much money; I had to set some on the side. Everyone else was counting their little dollar bills and I had hundreds and thousands!

Finally, about 1:00 a.m., they all went bankrupt and I won! They got up from the table with no word of congratulations and headed for bed. "Wait a minute, now!" I said. "Someone needs to put the game away." They replied: "That's your reward for winning. Good night!"

And there I sat, alone. All my hotels, all my deeds, all my money, and I realized, it doesn't amount to a thing. And I had to put them back in that box. Fold it up and put it on the shelf. And I went upstairs to a cold bed. My wife did not say, "You know, I'm so proud of you. You are such an impressive investor. We can never beat you. You are Mr. Monopoly." She just gave me a perfunctory kiss and turned over.[6]

Good thing, in Bob's case, his mistake was in a game. Too bad, in many cases, the mistake comes in life.

So don't be impressed with those who get rich and pile up fame and fortune. They can't take it with them; fame and fortune all get left behind. Just when they think they've arrived and folks praise them because they've made good, they enter the family burial plot where they'll never see sunshine again. We aren't immortal. We don't last long. Like our dogs, we age and weaken. And die. (Ps. 49:16–20 MSG)

God owns everything and gives us all things to enjoy. He is a good shepherd to us, his little flock. Trust him, not stuff. Move from the fear of scarcity to the comfort of provision. Less hoarding, more sharing. "Do good . . . be rich in good works, ready to give, willing to share."

And, most of all, replace fear of the coming winter with faith in the living God. After all, it's just Monopoly money. It all goes back in the box when the game is over.

■ ■ ■ ■

CHAPTER 10
SCARED TO DEATH

■ ■ ■ ■

Don't let your hearts be troubled. Trust in God, and trust also in me. . . . I will come and get you, so that you will always be with me where I am.

— JOHN 14:1, 3 NLT

FEAR OF LIFE'S FINAL MOMENTS

Once, in a dream, I encountered a man who was wearing a fedora and a corduroy coat. He was the classroom version of Indiana Jones: distinguished, professorial, strong jawed, and kind eyed. He frequented funerals. Apparently I did as well, for the dream consisted of one memorial after another — at funeral homes, chapels, gravesides. He never removed his hat. I never asked him why he wore it, but I did ask him to explain his proverbial presence at interments.

"I come to take people to their eternal home." In waking moments this explanation would have prompted a call to the FBI for a background check. But this was a dream, and dreams permit oddities, so I didn't probe. I didn't ask about the source of his list or the mode of his transport. I didn't think it odd to see the fedora at funerals. But I did think it strange to run into the man on a crowded street.

Think Thanksgiving Day parade or Fourth of July festival. A people-packed avenue. "I'm surprised to see you here," I told him. He didn't reply.

I saw one of my friends standing nearby. A good man, a widower, up in years, poor in health. Suddenly I understood the presence of the fedora-clad angel.

"You've come for my friend."

"No."

Then the dream did what only dreams can do. It dismissed everyone but the visitor and me. The crowded sidewalk became a quiet boulevard, so quiet I couldn't mistake his next words.

"Max, I came for you."

Curiously, I didn't resist, object, or run. I did, however, make a request. When he agreed, the street suddenly filled, and I began going from person to person, saying good-bye. I told no one about the angel or the hat or where I was going. As far as others knew, they would see me again tomorrow.

But I knew better, and because I did, the world righted itself. As if the lens of life had been out of focus, with a twist the picture cleared. Follies and offenses were forgotten. Love was amplified. I shook the hand of a harsh critic, gave my wallet to a beggar. I embraced a few coldhearted and hot-tempered folks. And to my dear ones, my wife and daughters, I gave a prayer. A more simple prayer I could not have prayed. *Stay strong. Trust Christ.*

And then the dream was done. I was awake. And within an hour I had recorded every memory of the dream.

It's lingered with me for years. Like a favorite song or sweater, I return to it. Can't say I do the same with other dreams. But this one stands out because it resonates with a deep desire that you might share: a desire to face death unafraid. To die without fright or a fight . . . perhaps with a smile.

Impossible? Some have said so.

Aristotle called death the thing to be feared most because "it appears to be the end of everything."[1] Jean-Paul Sartre asserted that death "removes all meaning from life."[2] Robert Green Ingersoll, one of America's most outspoken agnostics, could offer no words of hope at his brother's funeral. He said, "Life is a narrow vale between the cold and barren peaks of two eternities. We strive in vain to look beyond the heights."[3] The pessimism of French philosopher François Rabelais was equally arctic. He made this sentence his final one: "I am going to the great Perhaps."[4] Shakespeare described the afterlife with the gloomiest of terms in Hamlet's line: "The dread of something after death, the undiscover'd country from whose bourn no traveller returns."[5]

Such sad, depressing language! If death is nothing more than "the end of everything," "barren peaks," and "the great Perhaps," what is the possibility of dying bravely? But what if the philosophers missed it? Suppose death is different from how they thought of it, less a curse and more a passageway, not a crisis to be avoided but a corner to be turned? What if the cemetery is not the dominion of the Grim Reaper but the domain of the Soul Keeper, who will someday announce, "O dwellers in the dust, awake and sing for joy!" (Isa. 26:19 RSV)?

This is the promise of Christ: "Don't let your hearts be troubled. Trust in God, and trust also in me. There is more than enough room in my Father's home. If this were not so, would I have told you that I am going to prepare a place for you? When everything is ready, I will come and get you, so that you will always be with me where I am" (John 14:1–3 NLT).

While Jesus' words sound comforting to us, they sounded radical to his first-century audience. He was promising to accomplish a feat no one dared envision or imagine. He would return from the dead and rescue his followers from the grave.

Traditional Judaism was divided on the topic of resurrection. "For Sadducees say that there is no resurrection — and no angel or spirit; but the Pharisees confess both" (Acts 23:8). The Sadducees saw the grave as a tragic, one-way trip into Sheol. No escape. No hope. No possibility of parole. "The living know that they will die, but the dead know nothing" (Eccl. 9:5 NIV).

The Pharisees envisioned a resurrection, yet the resurrection was spiritual, not physical. "There are no traditions about prophets being raised to a new bodily life. . . . However exalted Abraham, Isaac, and Jacob may have been in Jewish thought, nobody imagined they had been raised from the dead."[6]

Ancient Greek philosophy used different language but resulted in identical despair. Their map of death included the River Styx and the boatman Charon. Upon death, the soul of the individual would be ferried across the river and released into a sunless afterlife of bodiless spirits, shades, and shadows.

This was the landscape into which Jesus entered. Yet he walked into this swamp of uncertainty and built a sturdy bridge. He promised, not just an afterlife, but a better life.

"There are many rooms in my Father's home, and I am going to prepare a place for you." We Westerners might miss the wedding images, but you can bet your sweet chuppah that Jesus' listeners didn't. This was a groom-to-bride promise. Upon receiving the permission of both families, the groom returned to the home of his father and built a home for his bride. He "prepared a place."

By promising to do the same for us, Jesus elevates funerals to the same hope level as weddings. From his perspective the trip to the cemetery and the walk down the aisle warrant identical excitement.

This point strikes home in our home as we are in the throes of planning a wedding. I use the word *we* loosely. Denalyn and our daughter Jenna are planning the wedding. I'm smiling and nodding and signing the checks. Our house bustles with talk of bridal gowns, wedding cakes, invitations, and receptions. The date is set, church reserved, and excitement high. Weddings are great news!

So, says Jesus, are burials. Both celebrate a new era, name, and home. In both the groom walks the bride away on his arm. Jesus is your coming groom. "I will come and get you . . ." He will meet you at the altar. Your final glimpse of life will trigger your first glimpse of him.

But how can we be sure he will keep this pledge? Do we have any guarantee that his words are more than empty poetry or vain superstition? Dare we set our hope and hearts in the hands of a small-town Jewish carpenter? The answer rests in the Jerusalem graveyard. If Jesus' tomb is empty, then his promise is not. Leave it to the apostle Paul to reduce the logic to a single sentence: "There is an order to this resurrection: Christ was raised as the first of the harvest; then all who belong to Christ will be raised when he comes back" (1 Cor. 15:23 NLT).

Paul was writing to Corinthian Christians, people who had been schooled in the Greek philosophy of a shadowy afterlife. Someone was convincing them that corpses couldn't be raised, neither theirs nor Christ's. The apostle couldn't bear such a thought. "Let me go over the Message with you one final time" (1 Cor. 15:1 MSG). With the insistence of an attorney in closing arguments, he reviewed the facts: "[Jesus] was raised from death on the third day . . . he presented himself alive to Peter . . . his closest followers . . . more than five hundred of his followers . . . James . . . the rest of those he commissioned . . . and . . . finally . . . to me" (1 Cor. 15:4–8 MSG).

Line up the witnesses, he offered. Call them out one by one. Let each person who saw the resurrected Christ say so. Better pack a lunch and clear your calendar, for more than five hundred testifiers are willing to speak up.

Do you see Paul's logic? If one person claimed a post-cross encounter with Christ, disregard it. If a dozen people offered depositions, chalk it up to mob hysteria. But fifty people? A hundred? Three hundred? When one testimony expands to hundreds, disbelief becomes belief.

Paul knew, not handfuls, but hundreds of eyewitnesses. Peter. James. John. The followers, the gathering of five hundred disciples, and Paul himself. They saw Jesus. They saw him physically.

They saw him factually. They didn't see a phantom or experience a sentiment. Grave eulogies often include such phrases as "She'll live on forever in my heart." Jesus' followers weren't saying this. They saw Jesus "in the flesh."

When he appeared to the disciples, he assured them, "It is I myself!" (Luke 24:39

NIV). The Emmaus-bound disciples saw nothing extraordinary about his body. His feet touched the ground. His hands touched the bread. They thought he was a fellow pilgrim until "their eyes were opened" (Luke 24:31 NIV). Mary saw Jesus in the garden and called him "sir" (John 20:15 NIV). The disciples saw Jesus cooking fish on the shore. The resurrected Christ did physical deeds in a physical body. "I am not a ghost," he informed (Luke 24:39 NLT). "Handle Me and see, for a spirit does not have flesh and bones as you see I have" (24:39).

Jesus experienced a physical and factual resurrection. And — here it is — because he did, we will too! "Christ was raised as the first of the harvest; then all who belong to Christ will be raised when he comes back" (1 Cor. 15:23 NLT).

Aristotle was wrong. Death is not to be feared. Sartre was mistaken. Your last moment is not your worst. The Greek itinerary was inaccurate. Charon won't ferry you into oblivion. Five hundred witnesses left a still-resounding testimony: it's safe to die.

So let's die with faith. Let's allow the resurrection to sink into the fibers of our hearts and define the way we look at the grave. Let it "free those who were like slaves

all their lives because of their fear of death"
(Heb. 2:15 NCV).

Jesus grants courage for the final passage.
He did for Charles Lindbergh, the first
person to fly solo across the Atlantic Ocean.
When the pilot discovered he had terminal
cancer, he and his wife went to spend their
final days at his Hawaiian home. He engaged a minister to conduct his last rites
and wrote out these words to be read at his
burial service:

> We commit the body of Charles A. Lind-
> bergh to its final resting place; but his spirit
> we commit to Almighty God, knowing that
> death is but a new adventure in existence
> and remembering how Jesus said upon
> the cross, "Father, into thy hands I com-
> mend my spirit."[7]

Death — "a new adventure in existence."
No need to dread it or ignore it. Because of
Christ, you can face it.

I did. As heart surgeries go, mine was far
from the riskiest. But any procedure that
requires four hours of probes inside your
heart is enough to warrant an added prayer.
So on the eve of my surgery, Denalyn, I,
and some kind friends offered our share. We
were staying at a hotel adjacent to the

Cleveland Clinic in Ohio. We asked God to bless the doctors and watch over the nurses. After we chatted a few minutes, they wished me well and said good-bye. I needed to go to bed early. But before I could sleep, I wanted to offer one more prayer . . . alone.

I took the elevator down to the lobby and found a quiet corner and began to think. *What if the surgery goes awry? What if this is my final night on earth? Is there anyone with whom I should make my peace? Do I need to phone any person and make amends?* I couldn't think of anyone. (So if you are thinking I should have called you, sorry. Perhaps we should talk.)

Next I wrote letters to my wife and daughters, each beginning with the sentence "If you are reading this, something went wrong in the surgery."

Then God and I had the most honest of talks. We began with a good review of my first half century. The details would bore you, but they entertained us. I thanked him for grace beyond measure and for a wife who descended from the angels. My tabulation of blessings could have gone on all night and threatened to do just that. So I stopped and offered this prayer: *I'm in good hands, Lord. The doctors are prepared; the staff is experienced. But even with the best of*

*care, things happen. This could be my final
night in this version of life, and I'd like you to
know, if that's the case, I'm okay.*

And I went to bed. And slept like a baby.
As things turned out, no angel came. I saw
no fedora. I recovered from the surgery, and
here I am, strong as ever, still pounding
away at the computer keyboard. One thing
is different, though. This matter of dying
bravely?

I think I will.

May you do the same.

■ ■ ■ ■

CHAPTER 11
CAFFEINATED LIFE

■ ■ ■ ■

I am leaving you with a gift — peace of mind and heart. And the peace I give is a gift the world cannot give. So don't be troubled or afraid.

— JOHN 14:27 NLT

Fear of What's Next

If only we could order life the way we order gourmet coffee. Wouldn't you love to mix and match the ingredients of your future?

"Give me a tall, extra-hot cup of adventure, cut the dangers, with two shots of good health."

"A decaf brew of longevity, please, with a sprinkle of fertility. Go heavy on the agility and cut the disability."

"I'll have a pleasure mocha with extra stirrings of indulgence. Make sure it's consequence free."

"I'll go with a grande happy-latte, with a dollop of love, sprinkled with Caribbean retirement."

Take me to *that* coffee shop. Too bad it doesn't exist. Truth is, life often hands us a concoction entirely different from the one we requested. Ever feel as though the barista-from-above called your name and handed you a cup of unwanted stress?

"Joe Jones, enjoy your early retirement. Looks as if it comes with marital problems and inflation."

"Mary Adams, you wanted four years of university education, then kids. You'll be having kids first. Congratulations on your pregnancy."

"A hot cup of job transfer six months before your daughter's graduation, Susie. Would you like some patience with that?"

Life comes caffeinated with surprises. Modifications. Transitions. Alterations. You move down the ladder, out of the house, over for the new guy, up through the system. All this moving. Some changes welcome, others not. And in those rare seasons when you think the world has settled down, watch out. One seventy-seven-year-old recently told a friend of mine, "I've had a good life. I am enjoying my life now, and I am looking forward to the future." Two weeks later a tornado ripped through the region, taking the lives of his son, daughter-in-law, grandson, and daughter-in-law's mother. We just don't know, do we? On our list of fears, the fear of what's next demands a prominent position. We might request a decaffeinated life, but we don't get it. The disciples didn't.

"I am going away" (John 14:28).

Imagine their shock when they heard Jesus

say those words. He spoke them on the night of the Passover celebration, Thursday evening, in the Upper Room. Christ and his friends had just enjoyed a calm dinner in the midst of a chaotic week. They had reason for optimism: Jesus' popularity was soaring. Opportunities were increasing. In three short years the crowds had lifted Christ to their shoulders . . . he was the hope of the common man.

The disciples were talking kingdom rhetoric, ready to rain down fire on their enemies, jockeying for positions in the cabinet of Christ. They envisioned a restoration of Israel to her days of glory. No more Roman occupation or foreign oppression. This was the parade to freedom, and Jesus was leading it.

And now this? Jesus said, "I am going away." The announcement stunned them. When Jesus explained, "You know the way to where I am going," Thomas, with no small dose of exasperation, replied, "No, we don't know, Lord. We have no idea where you are going, so how can we know the way?" (John 14:4–5 NLT).

Christ handed the disciples a cup of major transition, and they tried to hand it back. Wouldn't we do the same? Yet who succeeds? What person passes through life surprise free? If you don't want change, go to a soda machine; that's the only place you won't find any. Remember the summary of Solomon?

> For everything there is a season,
> a time for every activity under heaven.
> A time to be born and a time to die.
> A time to plant and a time to harvest.
> A time to kill and a time to heal.
> A time to tear down and a time to build up.
> A time to cry and a time to laugh.
> A time to grieve and a time to dance.
> A time to scatter stones and a time to gather stones.
> A time to embrace and a time to turn away.
> A time to search and a time to quit searching.
> A time to keep and a time to throw away.
> A time to tear and a time to mend.
> A time to be quiet and a time to speak.
> A time to love and a time to hate.
> A time for war and a time for peace. (Eccl. 3:1–8 NLT)

I count twenty-eight different seasons. Birth, death, lamenting, cheering, loving, hating, embracing, separating. God dispenses life the way he manages his cosmos: through seasons. When it comes to the earth, we understand God's management strategy. Nature needs winter to rest and spring to awaken. We don't dash into underground shelters at the sight of spring's tree buds. Autumn colors don't prompt warning sirens. Earthly seasons don't upset us. But unexpected personal ones certainly do. The way we panic at the sight of change, you'd think bombs were falling on Iowa.

"Run for your lives! Graduation is coming!"

"The board of directors just hired a new CEO. Take cover!"

"Load the women and children into the bus, and head north. The department store is going out of business!"

Change trampolines our lives, and when it does, God sends someone special to stabilize us. On the eve of his death, Jesus gave his followers this promise: "When the Father sends the Advocate as my representative — that is, the Holy Spirit — he will teach you everything and will remind you of everything I have told you. I am leaving you with a gift — peace of mind and heart. And the peace I give is a gift the world cannot give. So don't be troubled or afraid" (John 14:26–27 NLT).

As a departing teacher might introduce the classroom to her replacement, so Jesus introduces us to the Holy Spirit. And what a ringing endorsement he gives. Jesus calls the Holy Spirit his "representative." The Spirit comes in the name of Christ, with equal authority and identical power. Earlier in the evening Jesus had said, "I will ask the Father, and he will give you *another Counselor* to be with you forever" (John 14:16 NIV).

"Another Counselor." Both words shimmer. The Greek language enjoys two distinct words for *another.* One means "totally different," and the second translates "another just like the first one." When Jesus promises "another Counselor," he uses word number two, promising "another just like the first one."

The distinction is instructive. Let's say you are reading a book as you ride on a bus. Someone takes the seat next to yours, interrupts your reading, and inquires about the book. You tell him, "Max Lucado wrote it. Here, take it. I can get *another.*"

When you say, "I can get another," do you mean "another" in the sense of "any other" book? A crime novel, cookbook, or a romance paperback? Of course not. Being a person of exquisite taste, you mean a book that is identical to the one you so kindly gave away. If you had been speaking Greek, you would have used the term John used in recording Jesus' promise: *allos* — "another one just like the first one."

And who is the first one? Jesus himself. Hence, the assurance Jesus gives to the disciples is this: "I am going away. You are entering a new season, a different chapter. Much will be different, but one thing remains constant: my presence. You will enjoy the presence of 'another Counselor.' "

Counselor means "friend" (MSG), "helper" (NKJV), "intercessor, advocate, strengthener, standby" (AMP). All descriptors attempt to portray the beautiful meaning of *parakletos,* a compound of two Greek words. *Para* means "alongside of" (think of "*para*llel" or "*para*dox"). *Kletos* means "to be called out, designated, assigned, or appointed." The Holy Spirit is designated to come alongside you. He is the presence of Jesus with and in the followers of Jesus.

Can you see how the disciples needed this encouragement? It's Thursday night before the crucifixion. By Friday's sunrise they will abandon Jesus. The breakfast hour will find them hiding in corners and crevices. At 9 a.m. Roman soldiers will nail Christ to a cross. By this time tomorrow he will be dead and buried. Their world is about to be flipped on its head. And Jesus wants them to know: they'll never face the future without his help.

Nor will you. You have a travel companion.

You have a Pat McGrath. Pat is my biking buddy. A few years ago I took up road biking as a hobby and exercise. I bought the helmet, gloves, and thin-wheeled bike. I clipped my shoes in the pedals and almost died on the first ride. Hills are Everestish for the old and overweight. I literally had to walk my bike home.

Pat heard of my interest and offered to ride with me. Pat prefers biking to breathing. To him, biking *is* breathing. If he didn't have a job and five kids, the Tour de France might have known one more American. He has pistons for legs and a locomotive engine for a heart. When I complained about the steep roads and stiff winds, he made this offer: "No problem. You can ride on my wheel."

To ride on a biker's wheel is to draft on him. When Pat and I pedal into a stiff wind, I pull in behind him as close as I dare. My front wheel is within a foot of his rear one. He vanguards into the breeze, leaving me a cone of calm in which to ride. And when we bike up stiff hills? I'm a bit embarrassed to admit this, but Pat has been known to place a hand on my back and push me up the incline.

Couldn't you use such a friend? You have one. When you place your faith in Christ, Christ places his Spirit before, behind, and within you. Not a strange spirit, but the *same* Spirit: the parakletos. Everything Jesus did for his followers, his Spirit does for you. Jesus taught; the Spirit teaches. Jesus healed; the Spirit heals. Jesus comforted; his Spirit comforts. As Jesus sends you into new seasons, he sends his Counselor to go with you.

God treats you the way one mother treated her young son, Timmy. She didn't like the thought of Timmy walking to his first-grade class unaccompanied. But he was too grown-up to be seen with his mother. "Besides," he explained, "I can walk with a friend." So she did her best to stay calm, quoting the Twenty-third Psalm to him every morning: "Surely goodness and mercy shall follow me all the days of my life . . ."

One day she came up with an idea. She asked a neighbor to follow Timmy to school in the mornings, staying at a distance, lest he notice her. The neighbor was happy to oblige. She took her toddler on morning walks anyway.

After several days Timmy's little friend noticed the lady and the child.

"Do you know who that woman is who

follows us to school?"

"Sure," Timmy answered. "That's Shirley Goodnest and her daughter Marcy."

"Who?"

"My mom reads about them every day in the Twenty-third Psalm. She says, 'Shirley Goodnest and Marcy shall follow me all the days of my life.' Guess I'll have to get used to them."

You will too. God never sends you out alone. Are you on the eve of change? Do you find yourself looking into a new chapter? Is the foliage of your world showing signs of a new season? Heaven's message for you is clear: when everything else changes, God's presence never does. You journey in the company of the Holy Spirit, who "will teach you everything and will remind you of everything I have told you" (John 14:26 NLT).

So make friends with whatever's next.

Embrace it. Accept it. Don't resist it. Change is not only a part of life; change is a necessary part of God's strategy. To use us to change the world, he alters our assignments. Gideon: from farmer to general; Mary: from peasant girl to the mother of Christ; Paul: from local rabbi to world evangelist. God transitioned Joseph from a baby brother to an Egyptian prince. He changed David from a shepherd to a king. Peter wanted to fish the Sea of Galilee. God called him to lead the first church. God makes reassignments.

But, someone might ask, what about the tragic changes God permits? Some seasons make no sense. Who can find a place in life's puzzle for the deformity of a child or the enormity of an earthquake's devastation? When a company discontinues a position or a parent is deployed . . . do such moments serve a purpose?

They do if we see them from an eternal perspective. What makes no sense in this life will make perfect sense in the next. I have proof: you in the womb.

I know you don't remember this prenatal season, so let me remind you what happened during it. Every gestation day equipped you for your earthly life. Your bones solidified, your eyes developed, the umbilical cord transported nutrients into your growing frame . . . for what reason? So you might remain enwombed? Quite the contrary. Womb time equipped you for earth time, suited you up for your postpartum existence.

Some prenatal features went unused before birth. You grew a nose but didn't breathe. Eyes developed, but could you see?

Your tongue, toenails, and crop of hair served no function in your mother's belly. But aren't you glad you have them now?

Certain chapters in this life seem so unnecessary, like nostrils on the preborn. Suffering. Loneliness. Disease. Holocausts. Martyrdom. Monsoons. If we assume this world exists just for pregrave happiness, these atrocities disqualify it from doing so. But what if this earth is the womb? Might these challenges, severe as they may be, serve to prepare us, equip us for the world to come? As Paul wrote, "These little troubles are *getting us ready* for an eternal glory that will make all our troubles seem like nothing" (2 Cor. 4:17 CEV).

Eternal glory. I'd like a large cup, please. "One venti-sized serving of endless joy in the presence of God. Go heavy on the wonder, and cut all the heartache." Go ahead and request it. The Barista is still brewing. For all you know, it could be the next cup you drink.

■ ■ ■ ■

Chapter 12
The Shadow
of a Doubt

■ ■ ■ ■

"Why are you frightened?" he asked. "Why are your hearts filled with doubt?"
— LUKE 24:38 NLT

FEAR THAT GOD IS
NOT REAL

Woody Allen can't sleep at night. He is a restless soul. Fears keep the moviemaker, in his seventies, awake. To look at him, you'd think otherwise, what with his timid demeanor and gentle smile. He could pass as everyone's ideal uncle, polite and affable. His hair seems to be the only ruffled part about him. Yet beneath the surface, anacondas of fear nibble away.

The void overwhelms him. A strident atheist, Allen views life as a "meaningless little flicker." No God, no purpose, no life after this life, and, consequently, no life in this one. "I can't really come up with a good argument to choose life over death," he admits, "except that I'm too scared. . . . The trains all go to the same place. They all go to the dump."

So he makes films to stay distracted. For decades he's churned them out at the relentless pace of one a year. "I need to be focused on something so I don't see the big picture."[1]

I suppose someone exists who can't fathom Woody Allen's fears. There must be in God's great world a soul who has never doubted God's existence or questioned his goodness. But that soul is not writing this book.

My Woody Allen moments tend to surface, of all times, on Sunday mornings. I awake early, long before the family stirs, the sunrise flickers, or the paper plops on the driveway. Let the rest of the world sleep in. I don't. Sunday's my big day, the day I stand before a congregation of people who are willing to swap thirty minutes of their time for some conviction and hope.

Most weeks I have ample to go around. But occasionally I don't. (Does it bother you to know this?) Sometimes in the dawn-tinted, prepulpit hours, the seeming absurdity of what I believe hits me. I can remember one Easter in particular. As I reviewed my sermon by the light of a lamp, the resurrection message felt mythic, more closely resembling an urban legend than the gospel truth. Angels perched on cemetery rocks; burial clothing needed, then not; soldiers scared stiff; a was-dead, now-walking Jesus. I half expected the Mad Hatter or the seven

196

dwarfs to pop out of a hole at the turn of a page. A bit of a stretch, don't you think?

Sometimes I do. And when I do, I relate to Woody Allen's uneasiness: the fear that God isn't. The fear that "why?" has no answer. The fear of a pathless life. The fear that the status quo is as good as it gets and that anyone who believes otherwise probably invested in Juneau, Alaska, beachfront property. The chilling, quiet, horrifying shadows of aloneness in a valley that emerges from and leads into a fog-covered curve.

The valley of the shadow of doubt.

Perhaps you know its gray terrain? In it

- the Bible reads like Aesop's fables;
- prayers bounce back like cavern echoes;
- moral boundaries are mapped in pencil;
- believers are alternately pitied or envied; someone is deluded. But who?

To one degree or another we all venture into the valley. At one point or another we all need a plan to escape it. May I share mine? Those Sunday morning sessions of second-guessing dissipate quickly these days thanks to a small masterpiece, a wellspring of faith bubbling in the final pages of Luke's gospel. The physician-turned-historian dedicated his last chapter to answering one question: how does Christ respond when we doubt him?

He takes us to the Upper Room in Jerusalem. It's Sunday morning following Friday's crucifixion. Jesus' followers had gathered, not to change the world, but to escape it; not as gospel raconteurs, but as scared rabbits. They'd buried their hopes with the carpenter's corpse. You'd have found more courage in a chicken coop and backbone in a jellyfish. Fearless faith? Not here. Search the bearded faces of these men for a glint of resolve, a hint of courage — you'll come up empty.

One look at the bright faces of the females, however, and your heart will leap with theirs. According to Luke they exploded into the room like the sunrise, announcing a Jesus-sighting.

[The women] rushed back from the tomb to tell his eleven disciples — and everyone else — what had happened. It was Mary Magdalene, Joanna, Mary the mother of James, and several other women who told the apostles what had happened. But the story sounded like nonsense to the men,

so they didn't believe it. (Luke 24:9–11
NLT)

Periodic doubters of Christ, take note and
take heart. The charter followers of Christ
had doubts too. But Christ refused to leave
them alone with their questions. He, as it
turned out, was anything but dead and
buried. When he spotted two of the disciples
trudging toward a village called Emmaus,

Jesus himself came up and walked along
with them; but they were kept from recog-
nizing him. He asked them, "What are you
discussing together as you walk along?"
They stood still, their faces downcast. (vv.
15–17 NIV)

For this assignment angels wouldn't do,
an emissary wouldn't suffice, an army of
heaven's best soldiers wouldn't be sent.
Jesus himself came to the rescue.

And how did he bolster the disciples'
faith? A thousand and one tools awaited his
bidding. He had marked Friday's crucifixion
with an earthquake and a solar eclipse.
Matthew's gospel reveals that "saints who
had fallen asleep were raised; and coming
out of the graves after His resurrection, they
went into the holy city and appeared to
many" (27:52–53). Christ could have sum-

moned a few of them to chat with the Emmaus disciples. Or he could have toured them through the empty tomb. For that matter he could have made the rocks speak or a fig tree dance a jig. But Christ did none of these things. What did he do? "Jesus took them through the writings of Moses and all the prophets, explaining from all the Scriptures the things concerning himself" (Luke 24:27 NLT).

Well, what do you know. Christ conducted a Bible class. He led the Emmaus-bound duo through an Old Testament survey course, from the writings of Moses (Genesis though Deuteronomy) into the messages of Isaiah, Amos, and the others. He turned the Emmaus trail into a biblical timeline, pausing to describe . . . the Red Sea rumbling? Jericho tumbling? King David stumbling? Of special import to Jesus was what the "Scriptures said about himself." His face watermarks more Old Testament stories than you might imagine. Jesus is Noah, saving humanity from disaster; Abraham, the father of a new nation; Isaac, placed on the altar by his father; Joseph, sold for a bag of silver; Moses, calling slaves to freedom; Joshua, pointing out the promised land.

Jesus "took them through the writings of Moses and all the prophets." Can you imagine Christ quoting Old Testament scripture? Did Isaiah 53 sound this way: "*I* was wounded and crushed for *your* sins. *I* was beaten that *you* might have peace" (v. 5)? Or Isaiah 28: "*I* am placing a foundation stone in Jerusalem. It is firm, a tested and precious cornerstone that is safe to build on" (v. 16)? Did he pause and give the Emmaus students a wink, saying, "I'm the stone Isaiah described"? We don't know his words, but we know their impact. The two disciples felt "our hearts burning within us while he talked" (Luke 24:32 NIV).

By now the trio had crossed northwesterly out of the rocky hills into a scented, gardened valley of olive groves and luscious fruit trees. Jerusalem's grief and bloodshed lay to their backs, forgotten in the conversation. The seven-mile hike felt more like a half-hour stroll. All too quickly fled the moments; the disciples wanted to hear more. "By this time they were nearing Emmaus and the end of their journey. Jesus acted as if he were going on, but they begged him, 'Stay the night with us.' . . . As they sat down to eat, he took the bread and blessed it. Then he broke it and gave it to them. Suddenly, their eyes were opened, and they recognized him. And at that moment he disappeared!" (vv. 28–31 NLT).

Jesus taught the Word and broke the bread, and then like a mist on a July morning, he was gone. The Emmaus men weren't far behind. The pair dropped the broken loaf, grabbed their broken dreams, raced back to Jerusalem, and burst in on the apostles. They blurted out their discovery, only to be interrupted and upstaged by Jesus himself.

And just as they were telling about it, Jesus himself was suddenly standing there among them. "Peace be with you," he said. But the whole group was startled and frightened, thinking they were seeing a ghost!

"Why are you frightened?" he asked. "Why are your hearts filled with doubt?"

(Don't hurry past Christ's causal connection between fright and doubt. Unanswered qualms make for quivering disciples. No wonder Christ makes our hesitations his highest concern.)

"Look at my hands. Look at my feet. You can see that it's really me. Touch me and make sure that I am not a ghost, because ghosts don't have bodies, as you see that I do." As he spoke, he showed them his hands and his feet.

Still they stood there in disbelief, filled with joy and wonder. Then he asked them, "Do you have anything here to eat?" They gave him a piece of broiled fish, and he ate it as they watched.

Then he said, "When I was with you before, I told you that everything written about me in the law of Moses and the prophets and in the Psalms must be fulfilled." Then he opened their minds to understand the Scriptures. (vv. 36–45 NLT)

The disciples didn't know whether to kneel and worship or to turn tail and run. Someone decided the moment was too good to be true and called Jesus a ghost. Christ could have taken offense. After all, he'd passed through hell itself to save them, and they couldn't differentiate between him and Casper's cousin? But ever patient, as he is with doubters, Jesus extended first one hand, then the other. Then an invitation: "Touch me." He asked for food, and between bites of broiled fish, Jesus initiated his second Bible lesson of the day. " 'Everything I told you while I was with you comes to this: All the things written about me in the Law of Moses, in the Prophets, and in the Psalms have to be fulfilled.' He went on to open their understanding of the Word of God, showing them how to read their Bibles this way" (Luke 24:44–45 MSG).

We're detecting a pattern, aren't we?

- Jesus spots two fellows lumbering toward Emmaus, each looking as if he had just buried a best friend. Christ either catches up or beams down to them . . . we don't know. He raises the topic of the garden of Eden and the book of Genesis. Next thing you know, a meal is eaten, their hearts are warmed, and their eyes are open.
- Jesus pays a visit to the cowardly lions of the Upper Room. Not a Superman-in-the-sky flyover, mind you. But a face-to-face, put-your-hand-on-my-wound visit. A meal is served, the Bible is taught, the disciples find courage, and we find two practical answers to the critical question, what would Christ have us do with our doubts?

His answer? Touch my body and ponder my story.

We still can, you know. We can still touch the body of Christ. We'd love to touch his physical wounds and feel the flesh of the Nazarene. Yet when we brush up against the church, we do just that. "The church is his body; it is made full and complete by Christ, who fills all things everywhere with himself" (Eph. 1:23 NLT).

Questions can make hermits out of us, driving us into hiding. Yet the cave has no answers. Christ distributes courage through community; he dissipates doubts through fellowship. He never deposits all knowledge in one person but distributes pieces of the jigsaw puzzle to many. When you interlock your understanding with mine, and we share our discoveries . . . When we mix, mingle, confess, and pray, Christ speaks.

The adhesiveness of the disciples instructs us. They stuck together. Even with ransacked hopes, they clustered in conversant community. They kept "going over all these things that had happened" (Luke 24:14 MSG). Isn't this a picture of the church — sharing notes, exchanging ideas, mulling over possibilities, lifting spirits? And as they did, Jesus showed up to teach them, proving "when two or three of you are together because of me, you can be sure that I'll be there" (Matt. 18:20 MSG).

And when he speaks, he shares his story. God's go-to therapy for doubters is his own Word. "Before you trust, you have to listen. But unless Christ's Word is preached, there's nothing to listen to" (Rom. 10:17 MSG). So listen to it.

Jack did.

We began with the story of one atheist. Can we conclude with the account of another? Jack summarized the first half of his life with an incident that happened in his teenage years. He arrived at Oxford University in Oxford, England, anticipating his first glimpse of the "fabled cluster of spires and towers." Yet as he walked, he saw no sign of the great campuses. Only when he turned around did he realize he was actually walking away from the schools, headed in the wrong direction. More than thirty years later he wrote, "I did not see to what extent this little adventure was an allegory of my whole life."

He was a militant nonbeliever, devout in his resolve that God did not exist, for no God could stand for such a disaster as we call human existence. He summed up his worldview with a verse from Lucretius:

Had God designed the world, it would not be
A world so frail and faulty as we see.

Dismissing God, he turned his attention to academics, excelling in each field he studied. In short order the dons of Oxford took him in as a respected peer, and he began to teach and write. Yet not far beneath the surface, his doubts were taking their toll. He described his mental state with words like *abject terrorism, misery,* and *hopelessness.* He was angry and pessimistic, caught in a whirl of contradictions. "I maintained God did not exist. I was also angry with God for not existing." Jack would have agreed with Woody Allen's assessment of life: that all trains go to the same place . . . to the dump. He likely would have passed his days chugging toward the darkness, except for two factors.

A few of his close friends, also Oxford dons, rejected their materialistic view and became God-followers and Jesus-seekers. He first thought their conversion was nonsense and felt no fear of being "taken in." Then he met other faculty whom he admired, highly regarded teachers such as J. R. R. Tolkien and H. V. V. Dyson. Both men were devout believers and urged Jack to do something he'd, surprisingly, never done. Read the Bible. So he did.

As he read the New Testament, he was struck by its chief figure: Jesus Christ. Jack had dismissed Jesus as a Hebrew philosopher, a great moral teacher. But as he read,

Jack began to wrestle with the claims this person made: calling himself God and offering to forgive people of their sins. Jesus was, Jack concluded, either deluded, deceptive, or the very one he claimed to be, the Son of God.

On the evening of September 19, 1931, Jack and his two colleagues, Tolkien and Dyson, enjoyed a long walk through the beech trees and pathways of the Oxford campus — an Emmaus walk, of sorts. For, as they strolled, they rehashed the claims of Christ and the meaning of life. They talked late into the night. Jack, C. S. "Jack" Lewis, would later recall a rush of wind that caused the first leaves to fall — a sudden breeze, which possibly came to symbolize for him the Holy Spirit. Soon after that night Lewis became a believer. He "began to know what life really is and what would have been lost by missing it." The change revolutionized his world and, consequently, the worlds of millions of readers.[2]

What caused C. S. Lewis, a gifted, brilliant, hard-core atheist, to follow Christ? Simple. He came in touch with Christ's body, his followers, and in tune with his story, the Scriptures.

Could it be this simple? Could the chasm between doubt and faith be spanned with

Scripture and fellowship? Find out for yourself. Next time the shadows come, immerse yourself in the ancient stories of Moses, the prayers of David, the testimonies of the Gospels, and the epistles of Paul. Join with other seekers, and make daily walks to Emmaus. And if a kind stranger joins you on the road with wise teaching . . . consider inviting him over for dinner.

■ ■ ■ ■

CHAPTER 13
WHAT IF THINGS
GET WORSE?

■ ■ ■ ■

You will hear of wars and rumors of wars,
but see to it that you are not alarmed.
— MATTHEW 24:6 NIV

FEAR OF GLOBAL CALAMITY

I could do without the pharmaceutical warnings. I understand their purpose, mind you. Medical manufacturers must caution against every potential tragedy so that when we take their pill and grow a third arm or turn green, we can't sue them. I get that. Still, there is something about the merger of happy faces with voice-over advisories of paralysis that just doesn't work.

Let's hope this practice of total disclosure doesn't spill over into the delivery room. It might. After all, about-to-be-born babies need to know what they are getting into. Prebirth warnings could likely become standard maternity-ward procedure. Can you imagine the scene? A lawyer stands at a woman's bedside. She's panting Lamaze breaths between contractions. He's reading the fine print of a contract in the direction of her belly.

Welcome to the post–umbilical cord world. Be advised, however, that human life has been known, in most cases, to result in death. Some individuals have reported experiences with lethal viruses, chemical agents, and/or bloodthirsty terrorists. Birth can also result in fatal encounters with tsunamis, inebriated pilots, road rage, famine, nuclear disaster, and/or PMS. Side effects of living include super viruses, heart disease, and final exams. Human life is not recommended for anyone who cannot share a planet with evil despots or survive a flight on airplane food.

Life is a dangerous endeavor. We pass our days in the shadows of ominous realities. The power to annihilate humanity has, it seems, been placed in the hands of people who are happy to do so. Discussions of global attack prompted one small boy to beg, "Please, Mother, can't we go some place where there isn't any sky?"[1] If the global temperature rises a few more degrees . . . if classified information falls into sinister hands . . . if the wrong person pushes the wrong red button . . . What if things only get worse?

Christ tells us that they will. He predicts spiritual bailouts, ecological turmoil, and worldwide persecution. Yet in the midst of it all, he contends bravery is still an option.

"Watch out that no one deceives you. For many will come in my name, claiming, 'I am the Christ,' and will deceive many. You will hear of wars and rumors of wars, but see to it that you are not alarmed. Such things must happen, but the end is still to come. Nation will rise against nation, and kingdom against kingdom. There will be famines and earthquakes in various places. All these are the beginning of birth pains.

"Then you will be handed over to be persecuted and put to death, and you will be hated by all nations because of me. At that time many will turn away from the faith and will betray and hate each other, and many false prophets will appear and deceive many people. Because of the increase of wickedness, the love of most will grow cold, but he who stands firm to the end will be saved. And this gospel of the kingdom will be preached in the whole world as a testimony to all nations, and then the end will come." (Matt. 24:4–14 NIV)

Things are going to get bad, really bad,

before they get better. And when conditions worsen, "See to it that you are not alarmed" (v. 6 NIV). Jesus chose a stout term for *alarmed* that he used on no other occasion. It means "to wail, to cry aloud," as if Jesus counseled the disciples, "Don't freak out when bad stuff happens."

The disciples were making a big to-do over the buildings of the Jerusalem temple. Impressed with the massive hewed stones — some of them nearly twenty-four feet long — the followers applauded the awesome structure with its variegated marble that resembled the waves of the sea. Jesus was not so impressed. " 'Do you see all these things?' he asked. 'I tell you the truth, not one stone here will be left on another; every one will be thrown down' " (Matt. 24:2 NIV).

Imagine someone forecasting the collapse of the White House, Buckingham Palace, or the Louvre. Wouldn't you want some details? The disciples did. "Tell us, when will these things be? And what will be the sign of Your coming, and of the end of the age?" (v. 3).

Sitting on the Mount of Olives, in full view of the temple and the City of David, Jesus issued a "buckle your seat belt, no kidding, life can be fatal to your health" warning.

He began with "Watch out that no one deceives you. For many will come in my name, claiming, 'I am the Christ,' and will deceive many" (vv. 4–5 NIV). Note the twofold appearance of the word *many*. Many deceived and many deceivers. Churches are petri dishes for self-serving egomaniacs who masquerade as ministers of God. They will do so "in his name," claiming a special status, a superior spirituality. They boast of insider information and adorn their teaching with phrases like "God told me . . . ," "God spoke to me . . . ," "God led me . . ." They present themselves as religious gurus, code breakers, members of an inner circle, implying that they have access to knowledge unavailable to the common person. Some even position themselves as Jesus himself, "saying, 'I am the Christ' " (v. 5).

Jose Luis de Jesus Miranda is among them. He does not merely talk about or pray to Jesus. This man claims to be Jesus reincarnate. Unlike Jesus of Nazareth, this would-be Jesus from Puerto Rico teaches that there is no sin and that his followers can do no wrong. Thousands of adherents in more than thirty countries have swallowed his Kool-Aid.[2]

Don't be misled, Jesus warns. Don't be wooed by their slick appearances, silver-tongued oratory, or performances. Later in the same sermon Jesus said, "False Christs and false prophets will appear and perform great signs and miracles to deceive even the elect — if that were possible" (Matt. 24:24 NIV).

Multitudes and miracles. Large audiences and spectacular deeds. Throngs of people. Displays of power. When you see them, be careful. High volume doesn't equate with sound faith. Don't be impressed by numbers or tricks. Satan can counterfeit both.

Filter all messages and messengers through these verses: "And who is a liar? Anyone who says that Jesus is not the Christ. Anyone who denies the Father and the Son is an antichrist. Anyone who denies the Son doesn't have the Father, either" (1 John 2:22–23 NLT). False prophets always minimize the role of Christ and maximize the role of humanity. Be doctrinally diligent. Stick to one question — is this person directing listeners to Jesus? If the answer is yes, be grateful and pray for that individual. If the answer is no, get out while you still can.

Along with heresy we can expect calamity. "You will hear of wars and rumors of wars, but see to it that you are not alarmed. Such things must happen, but the end is still to come. Nation will rise against nation, and kingdom against kingdom. There will be famines and earthquakes in various places. All these are the beginning of birth pains" (Matt. 24:6–8 NIV).

Nature is a pregnant creation, third-trimester heavy. When a tornado rips through a city in Kansas or an earthquake flattens a region in Pakistan, this is more than barometric changes or shifts of ancient fault lines. The universe is passing through the final hours before delivery. Painful contractions are in the forecast.

As are conflicts: "wars and rumors of wars." One nation invading another. One superpower defying another. Borders will always need checkpoints. War correspondents will always have employment. The population of the world will never see peace this side of heaven.

Christians will suffer the most. "Then you will be handed over to be persecuted and put to death, and you will be hated by all nations because of me. At that time many will turn away from the faith and will betray and hate each other, and many false prophets will appear and deceive many people. Because of the increase of wickedness, the love of most will grow cold" (Matt. 24:9–12 NIV).

Paradise is populated with people whose deaths fulfilled this prophecy. Peter. Paul. Stephen. James. Ignatius of Antioch. Polycarp. Justin Martyr. Origen. The world hated these Christ-followers.

Hatred still abounds. Voice of the Martyrs, a Christian agency that defends religious liberties, contends that more Christ-followers have been killed for their faith in the last century than all previous centuries combined. The names of Paul, James, and Peter have been joined by Tsehay Tolessa of Ethiopia, Xu Yonghai of mainland China, Mehdi Dibaj of Iran.[3] The Global Evangelization Movement reports an average of 165,000 martyrs per year, more than four times the number of a century past.[4]

America, proud as she is of religious freedom, suffers from increasing anger toward Christians. Professors publicly mock Bible-believing students. Talk-show hosts denigrate people of faith. We can expect the persecution to increase. When it does, fragile convictions will collapse. "The love of many will grow cold" (v. 12 NLT). Spiritual stowaways will jump ship. The half-hearted will become coldhearted. A great many church attenders will be disclosed as faith pretenders. They will not only leave the faith; they will make the lives of the faithful miserable.

Will this persecution come to us? For some of you it already has. For many of us it might. If we are thrown into jail for our faith or deposed for our convictions, may God help you and me to remember the counsel of Christ: "See to it that you are not alarmed" (v. 6 NIV).

Don't freak out at the heresy, calamity, and apostasy. Don't give in or give up, for you'll soon witness the victory. "But he who endures to the end shall be saved. And this gospel of the kingdom will be preached in all the world as a witness to all the nations, and then the end will come" (vv. 13–14).

Jesus equipped his followers with far-sighted courage. He listed the typhoons of life and then pointed them "to the end." Trust in ultimate victory gives ultimate courage. Author Jim Collins makes reference to this outlook in his book *Good to Great.* Collins tells the story of Admiral James Stockdale, who was a prisoner of war for eight years during the Vietnam War.

After Stockdale's release Collins asked him how in the world he survived eight years in a prisoner-of-war camp.

He replied, "I never lost faith in the end

of the story. I never doubted not only that I would get out, but also that I would prevail in the end and turn the experience into the defining event of my life, which, in retrospect, I would not trade."

Collins then asked, "Who didn't make it out?" Admiral Stockdale replied, "Oh, that's easy. The optimists. . . . they were the ones who said, 'We're going to be out by Christmas.' And Christmas would come, and Christmas would go. Then they'd say, 'We're going to be out by Easter.' And Easter would come, and Easter would go. And then Thanksgiving, and then it would be Christmas again. And they died of a broken heart."[5]

Real courage embraces the twin realities of current difficulty and ultimate triumph. Yes, life stinks. But it won't forever. As one of my friends likes to say, "Everything will work out in the end. If it's not working out, it's not the end."

Though the church is winnowed down like Gideon's army, though God's earth is buffeted by climate changes and bloodied by misfortune, though creation itself seems stranded on the Arctic seas, don't overreact. "Be still in the presence of the LORD, and wait patiently for him to act. Don't worry about evil people who prosper or fret about their wicked schemes" (Ps. 37:7 NLT).

Avoid Pollyanna optimism. We gain nothing by glossing over the brutality of human existence. This is a toxic world. But neither do we join the Chicken Little chorus of gloom and doom. "The sky is falling! The sky is falling!" Somewhere between Pollyanna and Chicken Little, between blind denial and blatant panic, stands the level-headed, clear-thinking, still-believing follower of Christ. Wide eyed, yet unafraid. Unterrified by the terrifying. The calmest kid on the block, not for lack of bullies, but for faith in his older Brother. The old people of God knew this peace: "Though a host encamp against me, my heart shall not fear; though war arise against me, yet I will be confident" (Ps. 27:3 RSV).

After the bombs of World War II ravaged downtown Warsaw, only one skeletal structure remained on the city's main street. "The badly damaged structure was the Polish headquarters of the British and Foreign Bible Society, and the words on its only remaining wall were clearly legible from the street . . . 'Heaven and earth will pass away, but my words will never pass away.' "[6] This is the picture of the Christian hope. Though the world may collapse, the work of Christ will endure.

So, *see to it that you are not alarmed* (Matt. 24:6 NIV).

"*See to it . . .*" Bosses and teachers are known to use that phrase. "*See to it* that you fill out the reports." Or "Your essay is due tomorrow. *See to it* that you finish your work." The words call for additional attention, special focus, extra resolve. Isn't this what Christ is asking of us? In this dangerous day, on this Fabergé-fragile globe, with financial collapse on the news and terrorists on the loose, we have every reason to retreat into bunkers of dread and woe.

But Christ says to us, "See to it that you are not alarmed" (NIV).

"Keep your head and don't panic" (MSG).

"See that you are not troubled" (NKJV).

"Be faithful unto death, and I will give you the crown of life" (Rev. 2:10 RSV).

Make sure the hull of your convictions can withstand the stress of collisions.

Builders of the *Titanic* should have been so wise. The luxury liner sank because contractors settled for cheap rivets and suffered from poor planning. Rivets are the glue that hold the steel plates together. Facing a shortage of quality bolts, the builders used substandard ones that popped their heads upon impact with the iceberg.[7]

How sturdy are the bolts of your belief?

Reinforce them with daily Bible readings, regular worship, and earnest communion with God. "Courage is fear that has said its prayers."[8]

And remember: "All these [challenging times] are the beginning of birth pains" (Matt. 24:8 NIV), and birth pangs aren't all bad. (Easy for me to say.) Birth pains signal the onset of the final push. The pediatrician assures the mom-to-be, "It's going to hurt for a time, but it's going to get better." Jesus assures us of the same. Global conflicts indicate our date on the maternity calendar. We are in the final hours, just a few pushes from delivery, a few brief ticks of eternity's clock from the great crowning of creation. A whole new world is coming!

"These things must come to pass" (Matt. 24:6). *Must* is a welcome word that affirms that all events, even the most violent, are under a divine plan. Every trial and trouble has a place in God's scheme. "The reason why we ought not be terrified is not because wars are not terrifying. Quite the contrary. It is because above all chaos reigns a divine plan."[9]

All things, big and small, flow out of the purpose of God and serve his good will. When the world appears out of control, it isn't. When warmongers appear to be in

charge, they aren't. When ecological catastrophes dominate the day, don't let them
dominate you.

Let's trust our heavenly Father in the
manner Peter Wirth trusted his earthly one.

Peter was a twenty-one-year-old university
student when he began to experience severe
pain in his right shoulder. He called his
father for advice. Most students would do
the same: call home for counsel. But few
students have a better parent to call in such
a situation. Peter's father, Michael, is a
world-renowned orthopedic surgeon who
specializes in shoulders. Peter calling Dr.
Wirth with a shoulder problem is like Bill
Gates's daughter calling him with a software
question.

Michael initially attributed Peter's pain to
weight lifting. But after numbness and
tingling set in, the doctor grew suspicious
of an extremely rare shoulder condition
called deep venous thrombosis. A clot was
forming in his son's shoulder, dangerously
close to his heart. Michael was not only
acquainted with the condition; he had
coauthored the paper on how to treat it. He
sent Peter to the emergency room and told
him to request an ultrasound. Turns out,
Michael's long-distance diagnosis was right
on target. Peter was immediately admitted

to the hospital, where the clot was dissolved, and his earthly life was extended.

Wouldn't it be great to have such a father?

We do. He has diagnosed the pain of the world and written the book on its treatment. We can trust him. "Everything will work out in the end. If it's not working out, it's not the end."

CHAPTER 14
THE ONE
HEALTHY TERROR

They fell on their faces and were greatly afraid. But Jesus came and touched them and said, "Arise, and do not be afraid."
— MATTHEW 17:6–7

FEAR OF GOD
GETTING OUT OF
MY BOX

A woman in the hotel check-in line was holding one of my books under her arm. I was hesitant to introduce myself lest she explain that her doctor had prescribed the volume as insomnia treatment. But I took the risk. She actually said she liked it. But on second glance she didn't believe that I was who I claimed to be.

She flipped open the dust jacket, looked at my picture, then up at me. "You're not Max Lucado."

"Yes I am. The picture on the book was taken many years ago; I've changed."

With no smile she looked again at the photo. "No," she insisted, "Max Lucado has a mustache, no wrinkles, and a full head of hair."

"He used to," I explained.

She wouldn't budge. "He still does."

I started to show her my driver's license but opted to let her live with her delusion.

After all, if she wanted to remember me as a thirty-year-old, who was I to argue?

Besides, I understand her reluctance. Once you have someone pegged, it's easier to leave him there. She had me figured out. Defined. Captured. Freeze-framed in a two-by-three image. Max-in-a-box.

Boxes bring wonderful order to our world. They keep cereal from spilling and books from tumbling. When it comes to containing stuff, boxes are masterful. But when it comes to explaining people, they fall short. And when it comes to defining Christ, no box works.

His Palestinian contemporaries tried, mind you. They designed an assortment of boxes. But he never fit one. They called him a revolutionary; then he paid his taxes. They labeled him as a country carpenter, but he confounded scholars. They came to see his miracles, but he refused to cater. He defied easy definitions. He was a Jew who attracted Gentiles. A rabbi who gave up on synagogues. A holy man who hung out with streetwalkers and turncoats. In a male-dominated society, he recruited females. In an anti-Roman culture, he opted not to denounce Rome. He talked like a king yet lived like a pilgrim. People tried to designate him. They couldn't.

We still try.

My taxi-driving friend in Brazil kept a miniature Jesus superglued to his car dashboard. Anytime he needed a parking place or green light, he rubbed his plastic do-me-a-favor Jesus.

The preacher occupying the midnight broadcast time slot assured me and other late-night cable viewers that prosperity was only a prayer away. Just ask the make-me-a-buck Jesus.

I once reduced Christ down to a handful of doctrines. He was a recipe, and I had the ingredients. Mix them correctly, and the Jesus-of-my-making would appear.

Politicians pull box-sized versions of Jesus off the shelf, asserting that Jesus would most certainly vote green, conservative; often, never; like a hawk, dove, or eagle. The Jesus-of-my-politics comes in handy during elections.

Box-sized gods. You'll find them in the tight grip of people who prefer a god they can manage, control, and predict. This topsy-turvy life requires a tame deity, doesn't it? In a world out of control, we need a god we can control, a comforting presence akin to a lap dog or the kitchen cat. We call and he comes. We pet and he purrs. *If we can just keep God in his place . . .*

Peter, James, and John must have tried. How else can you explain this box-blowing expedition on which Jesus took them?

Now after six days Jesus took Peter, James, and John his brother, led them up on a high mountain by themselves; and He was transfigured before them. His face shone like the sun, and His clothes became as white as the light. And behold, Moses and Elijah appeared to them, talking with Him. Then Peter answered and said to Jesus, "Lord, it is good for us to be here; if You wish, let us make here three tabernacles: one for You, one for Moses, and one for Elijah." While he was still speaking, behold, a bright cloud overshadowed them; and suddenly a voice came out of the cloud, saying, "This is My beloved Son, in whom I am well pleased. Hear Him!" And when the disciples heard it, they fell on their faces and were greatly afraid. But Jesus came and touched them and said, "Arise, and do not be afraid." When they had lifted up their eyes, they saw no one but Jesus only. (Matt. 17:1–8)

The high points of Scripture seem to occur on the high points of earth. Abraham offering Isaac on Mount Moriah. Moses witnessing the burning bush on Mount Sinai. Elijah ascending to heaven from Horeb. Christ redeeming humanity on a hill called Calvary. And Jesus peeling back his epidermis on Mount Hermon.

No one knows for sure, but most historians place this event on a 9,200-foot-tall mountain called Mount Hermon. It towers over the northern Israeli landscape, actually visible from the Dead Sea a hundred miles away. This gigantic, snowy peak was the perfect place for Christ to retreat with Peter, James, and John. Away from the clamoring crowds and nagging controversies, Jesus could have the undivided attention of his three closest friends. Together they could look out over the turquoise-colored Sea of Galilee or the great plain, lumpy with vine-clad hills. Here they could pray. "He [Jesus] took Peter, John, and James and went up on the mountain to pray" (Luke 9:28). Christ needed strength. He was only months from the cross. The spikes of the soldiers and the spite of the crowd loomed ahead. He needed fortitude to face them, and he wanted his followers to see where he got it.

At some point while praying, the gentle carpenter who ate matzos and shish kebabs and spoke with a Galilean accent erupted into a cosmic figure of light. "He was transfigured before them. His face shone like the sun, and His clothes became as white as the light" (Matt. 17:2).

Light spilled out of him. Brilliant. Explosive. Shocking. Brightness poured through every pore of his skin and stitch of his robe. Jesus on fire. To look at his face was to look squarely into Alpha Centauri. Mark wants us to know that Jesus' "clothes shimmered, glistening white, whiter than any bleach could make them" (Mark 9:3 MSG).

This radiance was not the work of a laundry; it was the presence of God. Scripture habitually equates God with light and light with holiness. "God is light; in him there is no darkness at all" (1 John 1:5 NIV). He dwells in "unapproachable light" (1 Tim. 6:16 NIV). The transfigured Christ, then, is Christ in his purest form.

It's also Christ as his truest self, wearing his pre-Bethlehem and postresurrection wardrobe. Not "a pale Galilean, but a towering and furious figure who will not be managed."[1] One "who is holy, blameless, pure, set apart from sinners" (Heb. 7:26 NIV). A diamond with no flaw, a rose with no bruise, a song on perfect pitch, and a poem with impeccable rhyme.

In a flash Peter, James, and John were mosquitoes in an eagle's shadow. They'd never seen Jesus in such a fashion. Walk on water, multiply bread, talk to the wind, banish demons, and raise the dead, yes. But a standing torch? Turns out, Jesus was just getting warmed up.

Two visitors appeared: Moses and Elijah. The giver of the Law and the prince of the prophets stepped through the thin veil that separates earth from paradise. "They were speaking about his exodus from this world, which was about to be fulfilled in Jerusalem" (Luke 9:31 NLT).

Moses and Elijah, the Washington and Lincoln of the Jewish people. Their portraits hung in the entryway to the Hebrew Hall of Fame. And here they stood, the answer to Jesus' prayer. Don't we half expect Peter, James, and John to repeat their Sea of Galilee question: "What kind of man is this?" (Matt. 8:27 NIV)? The steward of the Law and the teacher of the prophets respond to his bidding?

About this point Peter cleared his throat to speak. Fire on the mountain became foot in the mouth. "Lord, it is good for us to be here; if You wish, let us make here three tabernacles: one for You, one for Moses, and one for Elijah" (Matt. 17:4).

These words might seem harmless to us, even a good idea to some. We like to memorialize moments with statues, tablets, or monuments. Peter thinks this event deserves a special building program and volunteers to head up the committee. Good idea, right?

Not from God's perspective. Peter's idea of three tabernacles was so off base and inappropriate that God wouldn't permit him to finish the sentence. "While he [Peter] was still speaking, behold, a bright cloud overshadowed them; and suddenly a voice came out of the cloud, saying, 'This is My beloved Son, in whom I am well pleased. Hear Him!' " (v. 5).

Beloved means "priceless" and "unique." There is none other like Christ. Not Moses. Not Elijah. Not Peter. Not Zoroaster, Buddha, or Muhammad. No one in heaven or on earth. Jesus, the Father declared, is not "a son" or even "the best of all sons." He is the "beloved Son."

Peter missed this. He placed Christ in a respectable box labeled "great men of history." He wanted to give Jesus *and* Moses *and* Elijah equal honor. God would have none of it. Christ has no counterparts. Only one tabernacle should be built, because only one person on the mountain deserved to be honored.

Peter, James, and John didn't speak anymore. No more talk of building programs.

No discussion of basilicas, tabernacles, memorials, or buildings. They were submariners reaching the Mariana Trench, astronauts landing on the lunar surface. They saw what no other people have seen: Christ in cosmic greatness. Words don't work in such a moment. Blood drained from their faces. Skin ashened. Knees wobbled and pulses raced. "They fell on their faces and were greatly afraid" (v. 6).

Fire on the mountain led to fear on the mountain. A holy, healthy fear. Peter, James, and John experienced a fortifying terror, a stabilizing reverence of the one and only God. They encountered the Person who flung stars into the sky like diamonds on velvet, who whisked prophets away in chariots and left Pharaoh bobbing in the Red Sea.

They were gripped deep in their gut that God was, at once, everywhere and here. The very sight of the glowing Galilean sucked all air and arrogance out of them, leaving them appropriately prostrate. Face-first on the ground. "They fell on their faces and were greatly afraid" (v. 6).

This is the fear of the Lord. Most of our fears are poisonous. They steal sleep and pillage peace. But this fear is different. "From a biblical perspective, there is nothing neurotic about fearing God. The neurotic thing is *not* to be afraid, or to be afraid of the wrong thing. That is why God chooses to be known to us, so that we may stop being afraid of the wrong thing. When God is fully revealed to us and we 'get it,' then we experience the conversion of our fear. . . . 'Fear of the Lord' is the deeply sane recognition that we are not God."[2]

How long since you felt this fear? Since a fresh understanding of Christ buckled your knees and emptied your lungs? Since a glimpse of him left you speechless and breathless? If it's been a while, that explains your fears.

When Christ is great, our fears are not.

As awe of Jesus expands, fears of life diminish. A big God translates into big courage. A small view of God generates no courage. A limp, puny, fireless Jesus has no power over cancer cells, corruption, identity theft, stock-market crashes, or global calamity. A packageable, portable Jesus might fit well in a purse or on a shelf, but he does nothing for your fears.

This must be why Jesus took the disciples up the mountain. He saw the box in which they had confined him. He saw the future that awaited them: the fireside denial of Peter, prisons of Jerusalem and Rome, the demands of the church, and the persecutions of Nero. A box-sized version of God simply would not work. So Jesus blew the sides out of their preconceptions.

May he blow the sides out of ours.

Don't we need to know the transfigured Christ? One who spits holy fires? Who convenes and commands historical figures? Who occupies the loftiest perch and wears the only true crown of the universe, God's beloved Son? One who takes friends to Mount Hermon's peak so they can peek into heaven?

Ascend it. Stare long and longingly at the Bonfire, the Holy One, the Highest One, the Only One. As you do, all your fears, save the fear of Christ himself, will melt like ice cubes on a summer sidewalk. You will agree with David: "The LORD is my light and my salvation; whom shall I fear?" (Ps. 27:1).

In the book *Prince Caspian,* Lucy sees Aslan, the lion, for the first time in many years. He has changed since their last encounter. His size surprises her, and she tells him as much.

"Aslan," said Lucy, "you're bigger."

"That is because you are older, little one," answered he.

"Not because you are?"

"I am not. But every year you grow, you will find me bigger."[3]

And so it is with Christ. The longer we live in him, the greater he becomes in us. It's not that he changes but that we do; we see more of him. We see dimensions, aspects, and characteristics we never saw before, increasing and astonishing increments of his purity, power, and uniqueness. We discard boxes and old images of Christ like used tissues. We don't dare place Jesus on a political donkey or elephant. Arrogant certainty becomes meek curiosity. Define Jesus with a doctrine or confine him to an opinion? By no means. We'll sooner capture the Caribbean in a butterfly net than we'll capture Christ in a box.

In the end we respond like the apostles. We, too, fall on our faces and worship. And when we do, the hand of the carpenter extends through the tongue of towering fire and touches us. "Arise, and do not be afraid" (Matt. 17:7).

Here's my hunch. Peter, James, and John descended the mountain sunburned and smiling, with a spring in their step, if not a slight swagger. With a Messiah like this one, who could hurt them?

Here's my other hunch. Mount Hermon's still ablaze and has space for guests.

■ ■ ■ ■

CONCLUSION: WILLIAM'S PSALM

■ ■ ■ ■

At 8:17 on the evening of March 3, 1943, bomb-raid sirens bansheed through the air above London, England. Workers and shoppers stopped on sidewalks and boulevards and searched the skies. Buses came to a halt and emptied their passengers. Drivers screeched their brakes and stepped out of their cars. Gunfire could be heard in the distance. Nearby antiaircraft artillery forces launched a salvo of rockets. Throngs on the streets began to scream. Some people threw themselves on the ground. Others covered their heads and shouted, "They are starting to drop them!" Everyone looked above for enemy planes. The fact that they saw none did nothing to dampen their hysteria.

People raced toward the Bethnal Green Underground Station, where more than five hundred citizens had already taken refuge. In the next ten minutes fifteen hundred more would join them.

Trouble began when a rush of safety seekers reached the stairwell entrance at the same time. A woman carrying a baby lost her footing on one of the nineteen uneven steps leading down from the street. Her stumble interrupted the oncoming flow, causing a domino of others to tumble on top of her. Within seconds, hundreds of horrified people were thrown together, piling up like laundry in a basket. Matters worsened when the late arrivers thought they were being deliberately blocked from entering (they weren't). So they began to push. The chaos lasted for less than a quarter of an hour. The disentangling of bodies took until midnight. In the end 173 men, women, and children died.

No bombs had been dropped.

Fusillades didn't kill the people. Fear did.[1]

Fear loves a good stampede. Fear's payday is blind panic, unfounded disquiet, and sleepless nights. Fear's been making a good living lately.

Here's a test. How far do you have to go to hear the reminder "Be afraid"? How near is your next "You are in trouble" memo? A flip of the newspaper page? A turn of the radio dial? A glance at the Internet update on the computer monitor? According to the media the world is one scary place.

And we suspect a campaign to keep it that way. Fear sells. Fear glues watchers to their seats, sells magazines off the racks, and puts money in the pockets of the system. Newscasts have learned to rely on a glossary of trouble-stirring phrases to keep our attention: "Coming up, the frightening truth about sitting in traffic." "How chocolate affects your I.Q." "What you can do to avoid the danger." "What you may not know about the water you drink."

Frank Furedi documented an increasing use of fear in the media by counting the appearances of the term *at risk* in British newspapers. In 1994 the term appeared 2,037 times. By the end of the next year, the total had doubled. It increased by half in 1996. During the year 2000 *at risk* was printed more than eighteen thousand times.[2] Honestly, did world danger increase ninefold in six years? We are peppered with bad news. Global warming, asteroid attack, SARS, genocide, wars, earthquakes, tsunamis, AIDS . . . Does it ever stop? The bad news is taking its toll. We are the most worried culture that has ever lived. For the first time since the end of the Second World War, parents expect that life for the next generation will be worse than it was for them.[3]

Even though life expectancy has doubled

and disease research is at an all-time high, you'd think the bubonic plague was raging in the streets. Reporter Bob Garfield tracked health articles in major publications and discovered that, among other health issues,

- 59 million Americans have heart disease,
- 53 million Americans have migraines,
- 25 million Americans have osteoporosis,
- 16 million struggle with obesity,
- 3 million have cancer,
- 2 million have severe brain disorders.

Reportedly, in total, 543 million Americans consider themselves to be seriously sick, a troubling figure since there are 266 million people in the country. As Garfield noted, "Either as a society we are doomed, or someone is seriously double-dipping."[4]

There's a stampede of fear out there. Let's not get caught in it. Let's be among those who stay calm. Let's recognize danger but not be overwhelmed. Acknowledge threats but refuse to be defined by them. Let others breathe the polluted air of anxiety, not us. Let's be numbered among those who hear a different voice, God's. Enough of these shouts of despair, wails of doom. Why pay heed to the doomsdayer on Wall Street or the purveyor of gloom in the newspaper? We will incline our ears elsewhere: upward. We will turn to our Maker, and because we do, we will fear less.

Courage does not panic; it prays. Courage does not bemoan; it believes. Courage does not languish; it listens. It listens to the voice of God calling through Scripture, "Fear not!" It hears Christ's voice comforting through the hospital corridors, graveyards, and war zones:

Be of good cheer; your sins are forgiven. (Matt. 9:2)

Be of good cheer! It is I; do not be afraid. (Matt. 14:27)

When reports come in of wars and rumored wars, keep your head and don't panic. (Matt. 24:6 MSG)

Let not your heart be troubled. (John 14:1)

Don't let your hearts be troubled or afraid. (John 14:27 NCV)

Do not fear therefore; you are of more value than many sparrows. (Luke 12:7)

Don't be afraid. (Luke 12:7 NIV)

We will follow the astounding example of William Fariss, who as a seven-year-old boy watched his house go up in flames. He is the son of Pioneer Bible translators in West Africa, a bright young man with a voracious interest in dinosaurs and animals. His family lived in a tin-roofed house covered by a layer of thatch. One day the wind lifted sparks from a nearby fire, and they exploded the Farisses' thatch roof in flames. The family attempted to save the house but stood no chance in the dry air and hot African sun. As they witnessed the fire reduce their home to cinders and charred brick, William's mother heard him praying. She noted that the words were psalm-like, and when she heard him repeat it a few days later, she wrote down what he said.

Through wind and rain
Through fire and lava
The Lord will never leave you.
Through earthquakes and floods
Through changing sea levels and burning
    ash
The Lord will never leave you.
If you love Him, He will bless you
and He will give you many things.

. . . .
Who can stop the Lord?
Who can chase a cheetah across the
plains of Africa?
The Lord, He can.
Who can stand on Mount Everest?
Who can face a rhinoceros?
The Lord.
The Lord can give you sheep and goats
and cows and ducks and chickens and
dogs and cats.
The Lord can give you anything He wants
to.

. . . .
Who can stop the Lord?
Who can face an elephant?
Who is brave enough to face a lion?
The Lord.
Who's as fast as a horse?
Who can catch a blue whale?
Who is brave enough to face a giant
squid?
The Lord.
Just as Jesus died on the cross, so the
Lord has done so.
The Lord will never leave His people.
The Bible is His word.
The Lord is a good leader.
. . . .
The Lord who loves you.

And He will not forsake His people.
The end.[5]

Though the flames threatened, the boy saw God in the flames. William trusted God and feared less. So can we.

Amen, William. And amen.

DISCUSSION GUIDE

This discussion guide for *Fearless* can be used either by groups or individuals who desire to gain a better grasp of the ideas and principles contained in the book. Each lesson consists of three parts:

- *Examining Fear,* in which you will revisit key portions of the text and will be asked to answer questions suggested by the quotations.
- *Exposing Fear,* in which you will spend time in selected Bible passages, pondering what God has to say on the topic.
- *Battling Fear,* in which one or two suggestions will be made for how to apply the lessons contained in that chapter.

CHAPTER 1
WHY ARE WE AFRAID?

Examining Fear

1. "Imagine your life wholly untouched by angst. What if faith, not fear, was your default reaction to threats? If you could hover a fear magnet over your heart and extract every last shaving of dread, insecurity, and doubt, what would remain? Envision a day, just one day, absent the dread of failure, rejection, and calamity. Can you imagine a life with no fear?"

A. Try to answer the questions above. How would your life be different today if all fear were erased from your heart?

B. Which are you more prone to — dread of failure, rejection, or calamity? What does that indicate about you?

2. "Getting on board with Christ can mean getting soaked with Christ. Disciples can expect rough seas and stout winds."

A. Why does getting on board with Christ mean getting soaked with Christ? Why doesn't it mean blue skies and clear sailing?

B. Why do so many believers *not* expect rough seas and stout winds? What often happens to them when they have to weather such conditions? How would you counsel them?

3. "Fear corrodes our confidence in God's goodness. We begin to wonder if love lives in heaven."

A. How does fear corrode our confidence in God's goodness? How has it done so in your own life?

B. When did you last wonder if love lives in heaven? Describe the circumstances.

4. "The fear-filled cannot love deeply. Love is risky. They cannot give to the poor. Benevolence has no guarantee of return. The fear-filled cannot dream wildly. What if their dreams sputter and fall from the sky? The worship of safety emasculates greatness."

A. Why does fear make it harder to love? Why does fear make it hard to give generously? How does fear stifle our dreams?

B. Have you ever found yourself worshiping safety? If so, what prompted you to do so? How does fear emasculate greatness? How has fear stopped you from attempting something great?

5. "The one statement Jesus made more than any other was this: don't be afraid."

A. Why would Jesus make this statement more than any other? What does this tell you about human nature?

B. How can you stop feeling afraid? What takes away the emotion of fear?

Exposing Fear

1. Read Matthew 8:23–27.

A. What connection does Jesus make between fear and faith in verse 26?

B. React to the following statement: "If Jesus is in your boat, whether he seems wide-awake or sound asleep, you have nothing to fear."

2. Read John 16:33.

A. What promise does Jesus give here about living in this world?

B. What does Jesus offer his followers? On what is this offer based?

3. Read 2 Timothy 1:7.

A. What kind of spirit has God *not* given to his children? What does this imply about the origin of most of our fears?

B. What kind of spirit *has* God given to his children? What difference should this make to us when fear strikes?

Battling Fear

1. Analyze your fears from this past week. What did they concern? What caused them? What did you do with them? How did you involve God in facing them? What patterns, if any, can you detect?

2. For one whole week meditate on 2 Timothy 1:7 in the translation of your choice. Repeat the verse in your head as often as you can.

CHAPTER 2
THE VILLAGERS OF STILTSVILLE
Fear of Not Mattering

Examining Fear

1. "Do we matter? We fear we don't. We fear nothingness, insignificance. We fear evaporation."

A. Do you ever fear that you don't matter to God? Explain.

B. How do you battle feelings of insignificance?

2. "Connect to someone special and become someone special, right?"

A. When are you most tempted to feel special by mentioning a personal connection you have to someone well-known or admired?

B. Why does the attempt to become someone special by connecting with someone special not make you feel any better in the long run?

3. "When the idea came through in the reading that the children in the Chinese orphanage are special simply because they were made by a loving creator . . . everyone started crying — including their teachers! It was wild."

A. How does the idea that you were made by a loving creator affect you? Do you feel special because of it? Explain.

B. Scripture says you are made in the image of God. What does that mean to you? If you were *not* made in God's image, would you act differently? Explain.

4. "The fear that you are one big zero will become a self-fulfilling prophecy that will ruin your life."

A. When are you most tempted to believe that you are one big zero? Describe the last time you felt this way.

B. How does fearing that you are one big zero become a self-fulfilling prophecy? Why will it ruin your life? What can you do about it?

5. " 'You matter already,' / he explained to

the town. / 'Trust me on this one. / Keep your feet on the ground.' "

A. Do you believe that you matter already? Explain.

B. What does it mean here to "keep your feet on the ground"? What would it mean for you to do this in your world?

Exposing Fear

1. Read Luke 12:4–7.

A. Of whom are we not to be afraid? Why not?

B. Whom are we to fear? Why? What kind of fear is meant?

C. What reason does Jesus give for not succumbing to fear (v. 7)?

2. Read Psalm 139:14–18, 23–24.

A. What kind of thoughts does God have toward you? How many thoughts does he have of you?

B. How do verses 14–18 give the psalmist the confidence to make his request in verses 23–24?

3. Read Ephesians 2:10.

A. Why did God create us? Why should this give us confidence?

B. Why can we feel confident that we can find God's best plan for us?

Battling Fear

1. Meditate on the crucifixion of Christ. What does the Cross say about how much you matter to God?

2. Imagine what life on earth might be like if God *didn't* care about men and women. What do you think would be different?

CHAPTER 3
GOD'S TICKED OFF AT ME
Fear of Disappointing God

Examining Fear

1. "Memories of dropped passes fade slowly. They stir a lonely fear, a fear that we have disappointed people, that we have let down the team, that we've come up short. A fear that, when needed, we didn't do our part, that others suffered from our fumbles and bumbles."

   A. What memory of a "dropped pass" haunts you the most?

   B. What do you typically do when such thoughts hit you? Do you dwell on them? Stew over them? Pray about them? Try to forget them?

2. "Might bravery begin when the problem of sin is solved?"

   A. How is sin a disappointment to God?

   B. Why would bravery begin with the solving of the problem of sin? What often fuels a lack of bravery?

3. "Adam and Eve did what fear-filled people do. They ran for their lives."

A. When you disappoint God and fear strikes, how do you run for your life?

B. When fear assaults you, what option is better than running? Why?

4. "God keeps no list of our wrongs. His love casts out fear because he casts out our sin!"

A. Why does God keep no list of our wrongs? How does that help you deal with the fear of disappointing him?

B. When you feel most loved by God, what happens to your fears? When you feel furthest from God, what happens to your fears?

5. "Nothing fosters courage like a clear grasp of grace. And nothing fosters fear like an ignorance of mercy."

A. How would you describe grace to someone who had never heard of it? How would you illustrate grace from your own life?

B. How has God shown you mercy? Where do you need his mercy most in your life right now?

Exposing Fear

1. Read Colossians 1:13–14.

    A. From what have believers in Christ been delivered or rescued?

    B. How have believers been redeemed? What does this redemption entail?

2. Read John 3:16–18, 36.

    A. Why did God send his Son into the world? What was *not* the Son's purpose?

    B. What is true of those who believe in the Son? What is true of those who do not believe in the Son?

3. Read John 6:37–40.

    A. Why did Jesus come down from heaven? What was his purpose?

    B. What is God's will for those who believe in his Son?

Battling Fear

1. Examine the scripture stories of these characters who disappointed God: Peter (Mark 14:27–31; John 21:15–19); David (2 Sam. 11); the Samaritan woman (John 4:1–42). How do their stories give you hope when you disappoint God?

2. Seek out someone whom you know to be a dedicated, enthusiastic believer in

Christ, and ask how he or she has battled the feeling of disappointing God.

CHAPTER 4
WOE, BE GONE
Fear of Running Out

Examining Fear

1. "Worry has more questions than answers, more work than energy, and thinks often about giving up."

   A. In what way does worry have more questions than answers? What sort of questions does it normally ask?

   B. Why does worry often think about giving up? When did worry last urge you to give up? What happened?

2. "Shortfalls and depletions inhabit our trails. Not enough time, luck, wisdom, intelligence. We are running out of everything, it seems, and so we worry. But worry doesn't work."

   A. What are you running out of that prompts you to worry?

   B. Why does worrying not help to deal with this lack? If worry doesn't work, then why do we worry?

3. "Legitimate concern morphed into toxic panic. I crossed a boundary line into the

state of fret. No longer anticipating or preparing, I took up membership in the fraternity of Woe-Be-Me."

A. How would you describe fretting? How does it differ from worrying? How susceptible are you to fretting? About what do you tend to fret the most?

B. How can you avoid taking up membership in the fraternity of Woe-Be-Me?

4. "Jesus doesn't condemn legitimate concern for responsibilities but rather the continuous mind-set that dismisses God's presence."

A. Where would you place the boundary between worry and legitimate concern for responsibilities?

B. How can you tell when you have developed a mind-set that continually dismisses God's presence?

5. "Standing next to the disciples was the solution to their problems . . . but they didn't go to him. They stopped their count at seven and worried."

A. Why do you think the disciples didn't immediately turn to Jesus?

B. Why do you suppose we don't immediately turn to Jesus when faced with a shortage of some kind?

Exposing Fear

1. Read Matthew 6:25–34.

    A. What reasons for not worrying does Jesus give in this passage?

    B. What are we to do instead of worrying about a lack of things? How does this work itself out in a practical sense?

2. Read John 6:1–13.

    A. What shortage faced the disciples? How did they respond to it? How did Jesus use it to expand their spiritual vision?

    B. How does verse 6 affect your understanding of this passage? What does it say about the very real shortages that you face?

3. Read John 15:7.

    A. What does it mean to abide or remain in Jesus?

    B. What does it mean for Jesus' words to abide or remain in you?

    C. What promise does Jesus make in this passage to those who follow his commands? How does the context affect your understanding of this promise?

Battling Fear

If you want to battle your fear of lack and instead enjoy a deep sense of *peacefulness*, then for at least one week try the following regimen:

1. **P**ray, first (1 Peter 5:7).
2. **E**asy, now (Ps. 37:7).
3. **A**ct on it (Matt. 25:14–28).
4. **C**ompile a worry list (Luke 10:41).
5. **E**valuate your worry categories (Matt. 6:25–27).
6. **F**ocus on today (Matt. 6:34; Heb. 4:16).
7. **U**nleash a worry army (1 Thess. 5:25).
8. **L**et God be enough (Matt. 6:28–33).

CHAPTER 5
MY CHILD IS IN DANGER
Fear of Not Protecting My Kids

Examining Fear

1. "The semitruck of parenting comes loaded with fears. We fear failing the child, forgetting the child. Will we have enough money? Enough answers? Enough diapers? Enough drawer space? . . . It's enough to keep a parent awake at night."

A. If you are a parent, what most worries you about taking care of your children?

B. How do you tend to deal with your fears about your children?

2. "Note to all panicking parents: Jesus heeds the concern in the parent's heart."

A. What examples of Jesus interacting with

parents or children can you remember? How did he treat them? What does that tell you about his heart for you and your children?

B. In what areas of dealing with your children do you most need Jesus' help right now?

3. "Wise are the parents who regularly give their children back to God."

A. What does it mean to give your children back to God? Have you done this? Explain.

B. Why is it necessary to regularly give your children back to God? In what situations do you feel tempted to refuse to give your children back to God?

4. "Prayer is the saucer into which parental fears are poured to cool."

A. How does prayer cool parental fears?

B. How would you describe your prayer life regarding your kids?

5. "Horror called from one side. Hope compelled from the other. Tragedy, then trust. Jairus heard two voices and had to choose which one he would heed. Don't we all?"

A. Describe a situation with your children where you are hearing two competing voices right now.

B. How can you train yourself to listen consistently to the voice of Jesus rather than to other voices that call you to fear?

Exposing Fear

1. Read Luke 8:40–56.

A. What challenges stood in the way of Jairus's receiving help from Jesus?

B. How does this passage show that a delay in receiving an answer to a desperate prayer does not necessarily mean a no?

2. Read Romans 8:31–32.

A. How does it change things if you know God is for you?

B. What proof does the apostle Paul offer to show that God is more than willing to give you what you need?

3. Read Genesis 22:1–18; Hebrews 11:19.

A. What do you think of God's test of Abraham? How do you think he tests you regarding your children?

B. What conviction allowed Abraham to successfully pass this difficult test (see Hebrews 11:19)? Do you put this much faith in the promises of God? Explain.

Battling Fear

Pick at least two of the following promises from Scripture and memorize them, repeating them to yourself every day for a month. Note what this does to your level of fear regarding your children. Passages: Deuteronomy 4:40; 5:29; 30:19; Psalm 37:25; Proverbs 20:7; Acts 2:38–39.

CHAPTER 6
I'M SINKING FAST
Fear of Overwhelming Challenges

Examining Fear

1. "It is in storms that Jesus does his finest work, for it is in storms that he has our keenest attention."

   A. What storms have you encountered in life?

   B. Describe how you have seen Jesus in a storm.

2. "Had Christ strolled across a lake that was as smooth as mica, Peter would have applauded, but I doubt he would have stepped out of the boat. Storms prompt us to take unprecedented journeys."

   A. Do you think Peter would have stepped out of the boat had the water been as smooth as mica? Explain.

   B. What unprecedented journey has some

271

storm prompted you to take?

3. "We aren't to be oblivious to the overwhelming challenges that life brings. We're
   to counterbalance them with long looks at
   God's accomplishments. . . . Do whatever
   it takes to keep your gaze on Jesus."
   A. What overwhelming challenges face you
at this moment?
   B. Describe some of God's greatest accomplishments in your life during the past
year.
   C. What does it take for you to keep your
gaze on Jesus?

4. "Feed your fears, and your faith will
   starve. Feed your faith, and your fears
   will."
   A. How do you tend to feed your fears?
What does this do to your faith?
   B. How do you feed your faith? What happens when you do?
   C. What keeps you from feeding your
faith?

5. "Jesus could have calmed your storm long
   ago too. But he hasn't. Does he also want
   to teach you a lesson? Could that lesson
   read something like this: 'Storms are not
   an option, but fear is'?"

A. How has a life-storm deepened your walk with Christ?

B. What is the purpose of these storms?

Exposing Fear

1. Read Matthew 14:22–33.

A. How many times is some form of fear mentioned in this passage?

B. How did Jesus respond to each of these fears?

2. Read Matthew 28:18–20.

A. How does Jesus describe his position in verse 18? How should this help us battle our fear?

B. What promise does Jesus give in verse 20? How should this help us battle our fear?

3. Read Romans 8:35–39.

A. What about the love of Christ is meant to help us battle our fears?

B. How can we become victorious, "more than conquerors," even when facing overwhelming circumstances?

Battling Fear

Choose one action to take this week to help arm you in the battle against fear.

- Memorize scripture.

273

- Read biographies of great lives.
- Ponder the testimonies of faithful Christians.
- Make the deliberate decision to set your hope on Christ.

CHAPTER 7
THERE'S A DRAGON IN MY CLOSET
Fear of Worst-Case Scenarios

Examining Fear

1. "What's your worst fear? A fear of public failure, unemployment, or heights? The fear that you'll never find the right spouse or enjoy good health? The fear of being trapped, abandoned, or forgotten?"

A. Answer the question above.

B. Describe your physical and emotional response to this fear.

2. "How many people spend life on the edge of the pool? Consulting caution. Ignoring faith. Never taking the plunge. . . . For fear of the worst, they never enjoy life at its best."

A. In what areas of life have you been staying on the edge of the pool? Why?

B. What good things in life has your fear prevented you from enjoying?

C. Name one area of life in which you

would like to take the plunge.

3. "God would unleash his sin-hating wrath on the sin-covered Son. And Jesus was afraid. Deathly afraid. And what he did with his fear shows us what to do with ours. He prayed."

A. Why does God hate sin so much? Why did God unleash his wrath on the sin-covered Son? How did Jesus become sin-covered?

B. What kind of praying best battles fear? How did Jesus exemplify this kind of praying?

4. "Why assume the worst? As followers of God, you and I have a huge asset. We know everything is going to turn out all right."

A. What worst-case scenario have you encountered in your life so far? How did it turn out? In what ways did you see God act in the middle of it?

B. How do followers of Jesus know that everything is going to turn out all right? How does that knowledge help us in the here and now?

5. "Dare we believe what the Bible teaches? That no disaster is ultimately fatal?"

A. What Bible passages best say to you that no disaster is ultimately fatal? List a few.

B. Does your behavior match your belief? Explain.

Exposing Fear

1. Read Mark 14:32–42.

A. What was the worst-case scenario facing Christ? What made him so troubled and distressed?

B. How did he respond to it?

2. Read Hebrews 5:5–9.

A. How does verse 7 describe Jesus' experience on earth?

B. Why did even Jesus have to learn obedience (v. 8)? What does this suggest about our battling fear?

3. Read 2 Timothy 4:14–18.

A. What adverse circumstances caused Paul some real trouble? How did he respond to them?

B. How did the Lord himself respond to Paul's troubles? What does this suggest about the way he will respond to your troubles?

Battling Fear

1. Although it will be uncomfortable, pull back the curtains and expose your fears, each and every one. When you examine them in the sunlight, what happens?

2. Seriously evaluate your connection to and involvement with a healthy local church. Recognize that "a healthy church is where our fears go to die. We pierce them through with Scripture, psalms of celebration and lament. We melt them in the sunlight of confession. We extinguish them with the waterfall of worship, choosing to gaze at God, not our dreads."

CHAPTER 8
THIS BRUTAL PLANET
Fear of Violence

Examining Fear

1. "Contrary to what we'd hope, good people aren't exempt from violence."

A. What kind of violence have you experienced in this world?

B. Why do you think good people have no exemption from violence?

2. "He who sustains the worlds with a word directs demonic traffic with the same."

A. Why is it important to know that God sustains the worlds with a word?

B. How does God direct demonic traffic without participating in their evil deeds?

3. "Courage emerges, not from increased police security, but from enhanced spiritual maturity."

   A. How does enhanced spiritual maturity develop courage?

   B. How much courage do you think you have? What does this say about your level of spiritual maturity?

4. "Satan cannot reach you without passing through God."

   A. Does it comfort you to know that Satan cannot reach you without passing through God? Explain.

   B. Why do you think God sometimes allows Satan to reach you? What is God's purpose?

5. "Heaven's best took hell's worst and turned it into hope."

   A. Describe "heaven's best" and "hell's worst." Why was it inevitable that heaven's best would triumph?

   B. How did heaven's best turn hell's worst into hope? How does this hope affect you personally? Explain.

Exposing Fear

1. Read Genesis 50:15–21.

    A. What kind of violence had Joseph's brothers done to him (see Genesis 37:11–28)?

    B. How did Joseph interpret this violence (v. 20)? How did he try to lessen his brothers' fears? What lesson is here for us?

2. Read Daniel 3:1–29.

    A. Why were Shadrach, Meshach, and Abednego threatened with violence?

    B. According to verses 17–18, what stance did they take? What happened to them? As a result, how did Nebuchadnezzar respond?

3. Read Hebrews 11:35b 40.

    A. What kind of violence was directed against people of faith as described in this passage?

    B. What promise kept them going through all their troubles? How is that promise meant to keep us going as well?

Battling Fear

Jesus himself suffered tremendously at the hands of violent men. Memorize Hebrews 12:2–3. How did Jesus endure the cross? Take some extended time to meditate on what he did so that you won't become weary or discouraged in your own walk of faith.

CHAPTER 9
MAKE-BELIEVE MONEY
Fear of the Coming Winter

Examining Fear

1. "The rich man's error was not that he planned but rather that his plans didn't include God. Jesus criticized not the man's affluence but his arrogance, not the presence of personal goals but the absence of God in those goals."

A. How do you include God in your financial planning?

B. What tends to happen to personal goals divorced from God and his perspective?

2. "The resounding and recurring message of Scripture is clear: God owns it all. God shares it all. Trust him, not stuff!"

A. Why is it important to remember that God owns it all? What tends to happen when we forget this truth?

B. When can you tell that you've started to trust money more than God? What are some telltale signs?

3. "The abundance of possessions has a way of eclipsing God, no matter how meager

those possessions may be. There is a predictable progression from poverty to pride."

A. Why does an abundance of possessions tend to eclipse God?

B. Why does wealth often lead to pride?

C. Can a poor person also be addicted to money? Explain.

4. "Those who trust money are foolish. They are setting themselves up to be duped and dumped into a dystopia of unhappiness."

A. In what ways do we trust money? How does a love of money dupe people?

B. Why does trusting in money always lead to a dystopia of unhappiness?

5. "Replace fear of the coming winter with faith in the living God. After all, it's just Monopoly money. It all goes back in the box when the game is over."

A. How much do you fear the coming winter? How can you reduce these fears?

B. Does it help you to think of real money as Monopoly money? Why or why not?

Exposing Fear

1. Read Luke 12:16–21.

A. Why did God call the man in this story a fool?

B. What does it mean to be rich toward God? Do you have this kind of riches? Explain.

2. Read 1 Timothy 6:6–10, 17–19.

A. What kind of contentment is described in verses 6–8? How does one enjoy this kind of contentment?

B. Why does Paul condemn the desire to be rich? What is wrong with the love of money?

C. What instructions does Paul give to the rich in verses 17–19? What promises does he give them?

3. Read Proverbs 23:4–5.

A. What attitude are believers to cultivate regarding riches?

B. Why should believers not set their hearts on getting rich?

4. Read Mark 12:41–44.

A. Why is it significant that Jesus watched people put money into the temple treasury? What does this imply for us?

B. Why does Jesus single out the widow

for praise? What lesson is she meant to teach us?

Battling Fear

1. Regardless of your financial position, this week give generously — more than you can really afford — to some group or individual who advances the cause of Christ. Write in a journal how your giving affects you and your household.
2. Set a date with a financial planner to evaluate how you can best use the money God has given you.

CHAPTER 10
SCARED TO DEATH
Fear of Life's Final Moments

Examining Fear

1. "What if the cemetery is not the dominion of the Grim Reaper but the domain of the Soul Keeper, who will someday announce, 'O dwellers in the dust, awake and sing for joy!' (Isa. 26:19 RSV)?"

A. How would you answer the question above?

B. Describe your attitude toward your own death.

2. "Jesus promised, not just an afterlife, but a better life."

A. How would you describe the better life Jesus promised to his followers?

B. How much of this better life are you experiencing?

3. "Jesus elevates funerals to the same hope level as weddings. From his perspective the trip to the cemetery and the walk down the aisle warrant identical excitement."

A. Why should funerals give Christians as much hope as weddings?

B. Can you say you are excited about your own death? Explain.

4. "Let's allow the resurrection to sink into the fibers of our hearts and define the way we look at the grave."

A. How does one's attitude toward death reveal what he or she truly believes about the resurrection?

B. What are some practical ways you can let the resurrection sink into the fibers of your heart?

5. "Death — 'a new adventure in existence.' No need to dread it or ignore it. Because of Christ, you can face it."

A. Describe someone you know who dreads death.

B. Describe someone you know who tries to ignore death.

C. How can you face death through your faith in Christ?

Exposing Fear

1. Read John 14:1–3.

A. What commands does Jesus give in verse 1?

B. What promises does he make in verses 2–3? How are these promises designed to lessen our fear?

2. Read 1 Corinthians 15:20–27.

A. How does this passage view death?

B. How can this passage calm our fear of death?

3. Read Hebrews 2:14–15.

A. Who had the power of death? How did Jesus destroy both him and his power?

B. How can we be released from a fear of death? In what way is this fear a kind of bondage?

Battling Fear

Pick up a copy of Peter Kreeft's *Love Is Stronger Than Death* and/or Herbert Lockyer's *Last Words of Saints and Sinners.* What difference does a vibrant faith in Christ make when death comes calling?

CHAPTER 11
CAFFEINATED LIFE
Fear of What's Next

Examining Fear

1. "If only we could order life the way we order gourmet coffee. Wouldn't you love to mix and match the ingredients of your future?"

A. Answer the question posed above.

B. If you could mix and match the ingredients of your future, what would your future look like?

2. "When you place your faith in Christ, Christ places his Spirit before, behind, and within you. Not a strange spirit, but the *same* Spirit. . . . Everything Jesus did for his followers, his Spirit does for you."

A. Describe how you rely on Christ's Spirit as you daily walk in faith.

B. Why is it important to know that the Holy Spirit acts in your life just as Christ would?

3. "Change is not only a part of life; change is a necessary part of God's strategy. To use us to change the world, he alters our assignments."

A. Why is change a necessary part of God's strategy?

B. How has God altered your assignment? How might he be altering it right now?

4. "What makes no sense in this life will make perfect sense in the next."

A. Does it help you to know that what makes no sense in this life will make perfect sense in the next? Explain.

B. What things in your life right now make no sense? How can you move forward without being able to make sense of them right now?

5. "If we assume this world exists just for pregrave happiness, atrocities disqualify it from doing so. But what if this earth is the womb? Might these challenges, severe as they may be, serve to prepare us, equip us for the world to come?"

A. In what way could this earth be a womb? Do you think it is? Explain.

B. How have some of your own challenges perhaps equipped you for the world to come?

Exposing Fear

1. Read John 14:16–18, 26–27.

A. What promises does Jesus give us in

287

verses 16–18? How can these promises help us battle the fear of what's next?

B. What is the vital connection between verses 26 and 27? How does Jesus' peace depend on the Spirit's work? How is the Spirit working in your life?

2. Read Ecclesiastes 3:1–8.

A. List the times or seasons that everyone will have to walk through, according to this passage.

B. How does knowing ahead of time that we will face such times and seasons help lessen our fears about tomorrow?

3. Read 2 Corinthians 5:17.

A. How does Paul describe someone "in Christ"?

B. What is the result of being "in Christ"? How does this help battle fear?

Battling Fear

1. List the major fears you've had in the last five years. How many actually came to pass? What did you waste while worrying over nothing?

2. Write a page or two on how the difficulties and troubles of this world may, in fact, be preparing you for the world to come.

CHAPTER 12
THE SHADOW OF A DOUBT
Fear That God Is Not Real

Examining Fear

1. "As I reviewed my Easter sermon by the light of a lamp, the resurrection message felt mythic, more closely resembling an urban legend than the gospel truth. . . . I half expected the Mad Hatter or the seven dwarfs to pop out of a hole at the turn of a page."

   A. Describe a time when you doubted the resurrection message could be true.

   B. What seems most unbelievable about the resurrection message?

2. "Periodic doubters of Christ, take note and take heart. The charter followers of Christ had doubts too. But Christ refused to leave them alone with their questions."

   A. Under what circumstances are you most likely to become a periodic doubter of Christ?

   B. How has Christ helped you deal with your occasional doubts?

3. "What would Christ have us do with our doubts? His answer? Touch my body and ponder my story."

A. How do you normally respond to your doubts?

B. How can you touch Jesus' body and ponder his story? How does this help to combat doubts?

4. "Christ distributes courage through community; he dissipates doubts through fellowship. He never deposits all knowledge in one person but distributes pieces of the jigsaw puzzle to many."

A. How does Christ distribute courage through community and dissipate doubts through fellowship?

B. Are you active in a local church? In what ways do you serve and receive help there?

5. "What caused C. S. Lewis, a gifted, brilliant, hard-core atheist, to follow Christ? Simple. He came in touch with Christ's body, his followers, and in tune with his story, the Scriptures."

A. How does regular involvement with Christ's followers help you follow Christ better?

B. How does regular interaction with the Bible help you grow in your faith? How does it help you battle fear?

Exposing Fear

1. Read Luke 24:13–35.

   A. Why do you suppose Jesus pretended not to know what the two men were talking about?

   B. What did these two men cite as the most compelling reason for them to regain their hope in Jesus (v. 32)? What helps you regain your hope in Jesus in the midst of doubts?

2. Read John 20:24–29.

   A. Why did Thomas at first not believe his fellow disciples when they told him they had seen the Lord?

   B. How did Thomas come to believe again?

   C. Why does Jesus call "blessed" those who have not seen but yet have believed?

3. Read Romans 10:17.

   A. How does faith come, according to this passage?

   B. What does this imply about regular Bible reading and study?

Battling Fear

As Max writes, "Next time the shadows come, immerse yourself in the ancient stories of Moses, the prayers of David, the testimonies of the Gospels, and the epistles of Paul. Join with other seekers, and make daily walks to Emmaus." This week:

1. Immerse yourself in the great stories of the Bible that showcase God's power and love.

2. Get deeply involved with other believers who seek to glorify God.

CHAPTER 13
WHAT IF THINGS GET WORSE?
Fear of Global Calamity

Examining Fear

1. "Life is a dangerous endeavor. We pass our days in the shadows of ominous realities. The power to annihilate humanity has, it seems, been placed in the hands of people who are happy to do so."

A. What ominous realities have the most power to frighten you?

B. How do you think you'd feel if a nuclear bomb went off in some part of the United States?

2. "It was as if Jesus counseled the disciples, 'Don't freak out when bad stuff happens.' "

A. Do you have a personal action plan for dealing with bad stuff? Explain.

B. What have you learned from observing

the way others handle difficulties?

3. "False prophets always minimize the role of Christ and maximize the role of humanity. . . . Stick to one question — is this person directing listeners to Jesus? If the answer is yes, be grateful and pray for that individual. If the answer is no, get out while you still can."

A. Why do false teachers inevitably point people away from Jesus? To what do they generally direct the attention of others?

B. How well do you know Jesus? Would you be able to tell if someone was painting a false picture of him? Explain.

4. "All things, big and small, flow out of the purpose of God and serve his good will. When the world appears out of control, it isn't."

A. How can bad stuff serve God's good will? Describe a time in your life when bad stuff served God's good will.

B. How do you generally react when your world seems to be spinning out of control? How would you counsel yourself in such times?

5. "Everything will work out in the end. If it's not working out, it's not the end."

A. Do you agree with the statement above? Why or why not?

B. How can this statement bring comfort and alleviate fear?

Exposing Fear
1. Read Matthew 24:4–14.

A. How many times is some form of deception mentioned in this passage?

B. What does this tell you about knowing sound doctrine as a tool against fear?

2. Read Psalm 46:1–11.

A. What kind of fears do verses 2–3 and 6 mention? How does the psalmist counteract these fears?

B. How do verses 8–11 allay our fears of major catastrophes?

3. Read Psalm 27:1–10.

A. What types of human-caused disasters are mentioned in verses 1–3? How does the psalmist respond to them?

B. What confidence does the psalmist express in verses 5–10? How did he gain this confidence? What can we learn from his experience?

4. Read Revelation 2:10.

A. What kind of suffering is promised to

some believers?9

B. How can these believers overcome their fears of such suffering?

C. What does God promise to those who overcome their fears and remain strong in Christ?

Battling Fear

Write out the following statement and place it in a prominent location that you will see often (on your refrigerator, in your car, on your office desk, etc.): "Everything will work out in the end. If it's not working out, it's not the end."

CHAPTER 14
THE ONE HEALTHY TERROR
Fear of God Getting Out of My Box

Examining Fear

1. "When it comes to defining Christ, no box works."

A. Into what boxes have you tried to put Christ?

B. Why is it impossible to put Jesus Christ into a box?

2. "The transfigured Christ is Christ in his purest form. It's also Christ as his truest self, wearing his pre-Bethlehem and postresurrection wardrobe."

A. Why is the transfigured Christ "Christ in his purest form"?

B. How can a mental picture of the transfigured Christ change the way you respond to adversity?

3. "Christ has no counterparts. Only one tabernacle should be built, because only one person on the mountain deserved to be honored."

A. Do you believe that Jesus Christ has no counterparts? Explain.

B. Name another occasion when God emphasized that Christ should be honored over others.

4. "Fire on the mountain led to fear on the mountain. A holy, healthy fear. Peter, James, and John experienced a fortifying terror, a stabilizing reverence of the one and only God."

A. What kind of terror can fortify you in your faith? How can a true reverence of God give you stability in times of uncertainty and fear?

B. What Old Testament person also experienced fire on a mountain? How did it affect his view of God? How did it change his life?

5. "How long since you felt this fear? Since a fresh understanding of Christ buckled your knees and emptied your lungs? Since a glimpse of him left you speechless and breathless? If it's been a while, that explains your fears. When Christ is great, our fears are not."

A. Answer the questions above.

B. How does a vision of a great Christ diminish our fears?

Exposing Fear

1. Read Matthew 17:1–8.

A. Why do you suppose Jesus wanted his three closest disciples to see him transfigured just before his death?

B. How can fear be both healthy and holy? From where does this kind of fear come? What did Jesus mean when he told the disciples not to be afraid?

2. Read 1 Timothy 6:13–16.

A. What does it mean to you that God dwells in unapproachable light?

B. What impression do you suppose verses 15–16 are designed to have upon our minds? What kind of fear does this image generate and for what reason?

3. Read 2 Peter 1:16–19.

A. What impression did the Transfiguration make on Peter?

B. What application does Peter make in verse 19? How can his guidance lead us into a holy, healthy, helpful fear?

Battling Fear

Carefully study and compare the four major accounts of the Transfiguration found in the Bible: Matthew 17:1–8; Mark 9:2–8; Luke 9:28–36; 2 Peter 1:16–18. Make a list of the story elements you find there. Then take time to ponder not only the event of the Transfiguration but how it affected Peter, James, and John. And keep in mind the following statement from Max: "Stare long and longingly at the Bonfire, the Holy One, the Highest One, the Only One. As you do, all your fears, save the fear of Christ himself, will melt like ice cubes on a summer sidewalk."

CHAPTER 15
CONCLUSION
William's Psalm

Examining Fear

1. "Fear loves a good stampede."

A. In what way is fear contagious?

B. How can you avoid joining the stampede?

2. "We are the most worried culture that has ever lived. For the first time since the end of the Second World War, parents expect that life for the next generation will be worse than it was for them."
A. Why do you think our culture worries so much?
B. Do you expect that life for the next generation will be worse than it is for you? Explain.

3. "Let's be among those who stay calm. Let's recognize danger but not be overwhelmed. Acknowledge threats but refuse to be defined by them."
A. Describe some ways you can recognize danger but not be overwhelmed by it.
B. How can you make sure that threats will not define you or your behavior?

4. "Enough of these shouts of despair, wails of doom. Why pay heed to the doomsdayer on Wall Street or the purveyor of gloom in the newspaper? We will incline our ears elsewhere: upward. We will turn to our Maker, and because we do, we will fear less."

A. Would meditating on the *Wall Street Journal* or on the Bible give you more hope? Why?

B. How does fixing your eyes on your Maker help you fear less?

5. "The Lord will never leave His people. / The Bible is His word. / The Lord is a good leader. / The Lord who loves you. / And He will not forsake His people."

A. What does it mean to you that the Lord will never leave you or forsake you?

B. In what way(s) has the Lord been a good leader for you?

Exposing Fear
1. Read Proverbs 29:25.

A. What is the outcome of fearing people?

B. What is the outcome of trusting in God, despite one's fear?

2. Read Isaiah 8:12–14.

A. Against what fears did Isaiah caution his countrymen?

B. What fear were they to cultivate?

C. How would this righteous fear help them in the here and now?

3. Read Hebrews 13:5–6.

A. What reason does the writer give for

being content with whatever we have?

B. What promise does the writer give us?

C. How does he want us to respond to this promise?

Battling Fear

For one week meditate several times a day on a single verse of Scripture from God's own mouth: "I will never leave you nor forsake you" (Heb. 13:5). At the end of each day, spend at least ten minutes praising him for his eternal commitment to you.

NOTES

Chapter 1: Why Are We Afraid?

1. The Report Newsmagazine, January 22, 2001, Candis McLean. http://www.find articles.com/plarticles/m_hb3543/is_2001/01/ai_n8359052?tag=content;col1
2. Shelley Wachsmann, *The Sea of Galilee Boat: An Extraordinary 2000 Year Old Discovery* (New York: Plenum Press, 1995), 326–28.
3. Walter Brueggemann, "The Liturgy of Abundance, the Myth of Scarcity," *Christian Century,* March 24–31, 1999, http://www.religion-online.org/showarticle.asp?title=533.

Chapter 2: The Villagers of Stiltsville

1. Rabbi Shmuley Boteach, *Face Your Fear: Living with Courage in an Age of Caution* (New York: St Martin's Griffin, 2004), 21.
2. John Bentley, e-mail message to author.

Used by permission.

3. E-mail message to Women of Faith, September 6, 2008. Used by permission.

Chapter 3: God's Ticked Off at Me

1. Ken Rodriguez, "History Keeps Digging Its Horns into Texas Receiver," *San Antonio Express-News,* October 26, 2001.
2. Calvin Miller, *Into the Depths of God: Where Eyes See the Invisible, Ears Hear the Inaudible, and Minds Conceive the Inconceivable* (Minneapolis: Bethany House Publishers, 2000), 135.

Chapter 4: Woe, Be Gone

1. Bradford Torrey, "Not So in Haste, My Heart," *The Boston Transcript,* 1875, CyberHymnal.org, http://www.cyberhymnal .org/htm/n/s/nsinhamh.htm.

Chapter 6: I'm Sinking Fast

1. Shelley Wachsmann, *The Sea of Galilee Boat: An Extraordinary 2000 Year Old Discovery* (New York: Plenum Press, 1995), 39, 121.
2. C. S. Lewis, *Mere Christianity* (New York: Macmillan Publishing, 1952), 123–24. © C. S. Lewis Pte. Ltd. 1942, 1943, 1944, 1952. Extract reprinted by permission.

Chapter 7: There's a Dragon in My Closet

1. Joshua Previn and David Borgenicht, *The Complete Worst-Case Scenario Survival Handbook* (San Francisco: Chronicle Books, 2007).
2. Max Lucado, *No Wonder They Call Him the Savior* (Nashville, TN: Thomas Nelson, 2004), 105.
3. Pierre Benoit, *The Passion and Resurrection of Jesus Christ,* trans. Benet Weatherhead (New York: Herder and Herder, 1969), 10, as quoted by Frederick Dale Bruner, *Matthew: A Commentary,* vol. 2, *The Churchbook: Matthew 13–28* (Dallas: Word Publishing, 1990), 979.
4. Bruner, *The Churchbook,* 978.
5. Yann Martel, *Life of Pi* (Orlando, FL: Harcourt, 2001), 160. Copyright by Yann Martel. Reprinted by permission of Houghton Mifflin Harcourt Publishing Company.
6. Ibid.
7. Robert Wheler Bush, *The Life and Times of Chrysostom* (London, England: Religious Tract Society, 1885), 245.

Chapter 8: This Brutal Planet

1. From a conversation with Peggy Nelson. Used by permission.
2. Charles Colson, *Loving God* (Grand

Rapids: Zondervan, 1983), 27–34.

3. Martin Luther, "A Mighty Fortress," Hymnsite.com, http://www.hymnsite.com/lyrics/umh110.sht.

4. Rabbi Shmuley Boteach, *Face Your Fear: Living with Courage in an Age of Caution* (New York: St Martin's Griffin, 2004), 86.

5. Philip Gourevitch, *We Wish to Inform You That Tomorrow We Will Be Killed with Our Families: Stories from Rwanda* (New York: Farrar, Straus, and Giroux, 1998), 123.

6. Peter Lewis, *The Glory of Christ* (London: Hodder and Stoughton, 1992), 235.

7. Aleksandr I. Solzhenitsyn, *The Gulag Archipelago, 1918–1956: An Experiment in Literary Investigation,* trans. Thomas P. Whitney (New York: HarperPerennial, 2007), 309–12.

Chapter 9: Make-Believe Money

1. Michael P. Mayko, "Stamford Man Faces Federal Charges in Bomb Threat," *Connecticut Post,* October 9, 2008, http://www.connpost.com/archive?vertical=archive.

2. Walter Brueggemann, "The Liturgy of Abundance, the Myth of Scarcity," *Christian Century,* March 24–31, 1999, http://www.religion-online.org/showarticle.asp?title=533.

3. Anup Shah, "Poverty Facts and Stats," citing World Bank Development Indicators 2008, http://www.globalissues.org/article/26/poverty-facts-and-stats.
4. Thomas Carlyle, QuoteWorld.org, http://www.quoteworld.org/quotes/2411.
5. "The Politics of Investing," *Leading the Way: A Publication of Hartford Leaders Suite of Variable Annuities,* third quarter, 2008.
6. Bob Russell, "Favorites of Bob Russell," CD (Louisville, KY: Southeast Christian Church, 2005).

Chapter 10: Scared to Death

1. Donald G. Bloesch, *The Last Things: Resurrection, Judgment, Glory* (Downers Grove, IL: InterVarsity Press, 2004), 125.
2. Ibid.
3. John Blanchard, *Whatever Happened to Hell?* (Wheaton, IL: Crossway Books, 1995), 63.
4. Blanchard, *Whatever Happened to Hell?* 62.
5. William Shakespeare, *Hamlet,* in *The Complete Works of Shakespeare,* ed. Hardin Craig (Glenview, IL: Scott, Foresman and Company, 1961), 3.1.78–80. References are to act, scene, and line.
6. N. T. Wright, *Christian Origins and the Question of God,* vol. 3, *The Resurrection*

of the Son of God (Minneapolis: Fortress Press, 2003), 205–6.

7. Benjamin P. Browne, *Illustrations for Preaching* (Nashville, TN: Broadman Press, 1977), 85.

Chapter 12: The Shadow of a Doubt

1. Jennie Yabroff, "Take the Bananas and Run," *Newsweek,* August 18–25, 2008, 57.

2. Armand M. Nicholi Jr., *The Question of God: C. S. Lewis and Sigmund Freud Debate God, Love, Sex, and the Meaning of Life* (New York: Free Press, 2002), 84–92, 111–14.

Chapter 13: What If Things Get Worse?

1. Joanna Bourke, *Fear: A Cultural History* (Emeryville, CA: Shoemaker and Hoard, 2005), 195.

2. John Zarrella and Patrick Oppmann, "Pastor with 666 Tattoo Claims to Be Divine," CNN.com, February 19, 2007, http://www.cnn.com/2007/US/02/16/miami.preacher.

3. dc Talk and the Voice of the Martyrs, *Jesus Freaks* (Tulsa, OK: Albury Publishing, 1999), 133, 167, 208.

4. Global Evangelization Movement, "Status of Global Mission, 2001, in Context of 20th and 21st Centuries," Worldwide

Persian Outreach, http://www.farsinet
.com/pwo/world_mission.html.

5. Jim Collins, *Good to Great: Why Some Companies Make the Leap . . . and Others Don't* (New York: Harper Collins, 2001), 83–5.

6. Frederick Dale Bruner, *Matthew: A Commentary,* vol. 2, *The Churchbook: Matthew 13–28* (Dallas: Word Publishing, 1990), 878.

7. William J. Broad, "Scientists' New Findings Link Titanic's Fast Sinking to Rivets," *San Antonio Express-News,* April 15, 2008.

8. Dorothy Bernard, The Quotations Page, http://www.quotationspage.com/quote/ 29699.html.

9. Bruner, *The Churchbook,* 847.

Chapter 14: The One Healthy Terror

1. Thomas Howard, *Christ the Tiger* (Philadelphia: J. B. Lippincott, 1967), 10.

2. Ellen F. Davis, *Getting Involved with God: Rediscovering the Old Testament* (Cambridge, MA: Cowley Press, 2001), 102–3.

3. C. S. Lewis, *Prince Caspian: The Return to Narnia* (New York: Macmillan Publishing, 1951), 136. Copyright © C. S. Lewis Pte. Ltd. 1942, 1943, 1944, 1952. Extract

reprinted by permission.

Conclusion: William's Psalm

1. Joanna Bourke, *Fear: A Cultural History* (Emeryville, CA: Shoemaker and Hoard, 2005), 232–33.
2. Frank Furedi, *Culture of Fear Revisited: Risk-taking and the Morality of Low Expectation,* 4th ed. (New York: Continuum Books, 2006), xviii.
3. Ibid., 68
4. John Ortberg, *If You Want to Walk on Water, You've Got to Get Out of the Boat* (Grand Rapids, MI: Zondervan, 2001), 132.
5. Greg Pruett, "President's Blog," Pioneer Bible Translators, February 27, 2008, http://www.pioneerbible.org/cms/tiki-view_blog_post.php?blogId=2&postId=9.

ABOUT THE AUTHOR

Max Lucado, Minister of Writing and Preaching for the Oak Hills Church in San Antonio, Texas, is the husband of Denalyn and father of Jenna, Andrea, and Sara. In a good week, he reads a good book, has a few dinners with his wife, and breaks 90 on the golf course. He usually settles for the first two.

Visit his Web site at www.maxlucado.com.

The employees of Thorndike Press hope you have enjoyed this Large Print book. All our Thorndike, Wheeler, and Kennebec Large Print titles are designed for easy reading, and all our books are made to last. Other Thorndike Press Large Print books are available at your library, through selected bookstores, or directly from us.

For information about titles, please call:
  (800) 223-1244

or visit our Web site at:
  http://gale.cengage.com/thorndike

To share your comments, please write:
  Publisher
  Thorndike Press
  295 Kennedy Memorial Drive
  Waterville, ME 04901